The Journey of a Healer

Main Road and Side Roads

Maya Kraus

To: Lottie & Sophie, with Love, Maya

May the Universe guide you safely throughout your own life's Journey

The Journey of a Healer
Main Road and Side Roads

ISBN 978-1-849-14276-2

Second Edition 2013
First published in Great Britain 2012

Copyright Maya Kraus 2012

All rights reserved. No part of this publication may be reproduced, stored or introduced into a retrieval system, or transmitted, in any form, or by any means (electronic, mechanical, photocopying, recording or otherwise) without the prior written permission of the publisher.

This book is sold subject to the condition that it shall not, by way of trade or otherwise, be lent, resold, hired out, or otherwise circulated without the publisher's prior consent in any form of binding or cover other than that in which it is published and without a similar condition including this condition being imposed on the subsequent purchaser.

Cover artwork by Clare Hackney
Proof reading by Ruth Rayment

Book production, mentoring and support from Tom Evans
www.tomevans.co

For my courageous and brave parents and grandmother, Oma, who were so perfect

Also for my precious children Pamela, Simon and Oliver who always keep turning the wheel of my life with gaiety

Also from Maya Kraus

The Ten Qualities :
A Simple Guide to Well-being

PREFACE

I have come to realise how my life's experiences from childhood onwards have shaped my interest in natural healing and led to my becoming a natural health practitioner.

In setting down my story and sharing the knowledge I have acquired over twenty-five years of study and practice, I hope to offer some insight and enlightenment into the positive benefits that complementary medicine and therapy can offer.

My path has shown me how the innate wisdom of our body can help to guide and promote good health and lead to personal fulfilment. By sharing my story with you, my hope is that you will be encouraged to make your own investigations.

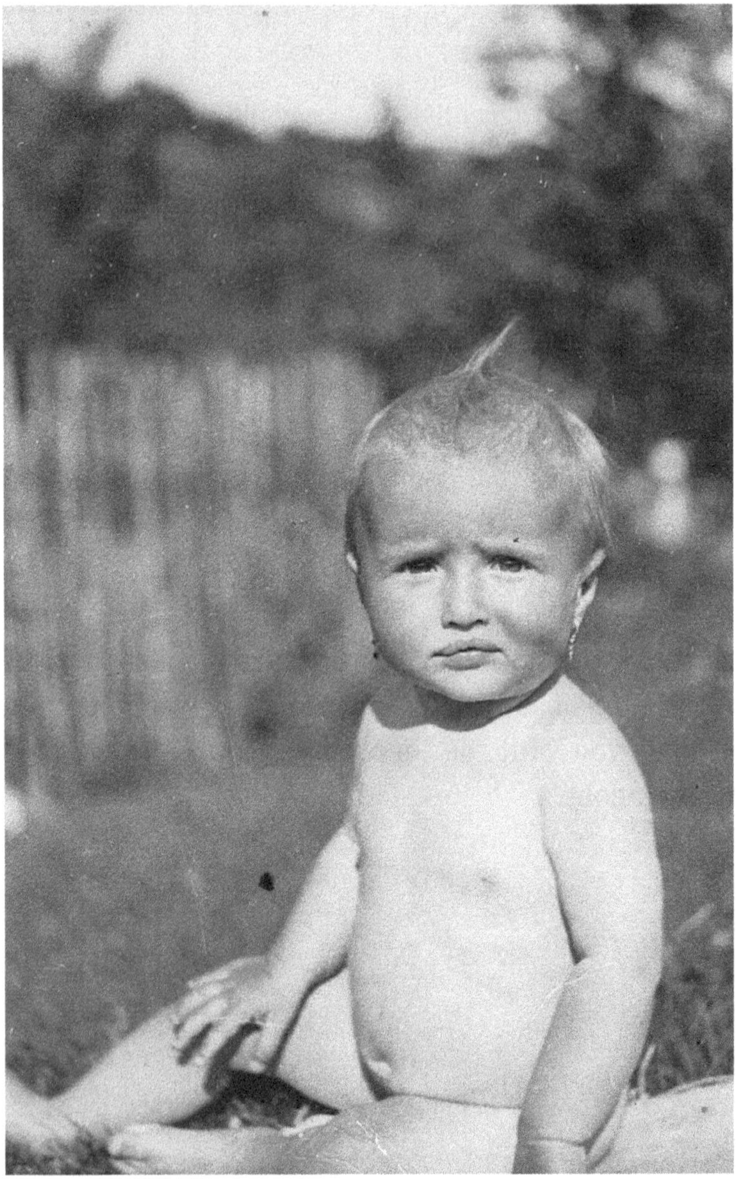

1. THE THOUSANDTH BABY

This is an account written to me by my grandmother about my birth.

One cold morning in late 1942, Anna Unger, the seventy-year-old midwife of Katharinaberg, a well-known fashionable ski resort in the Erzgebirge north of Czechoslovakia, set off with joy on what was going to be her very last celebration of birth. She had delivered 999 babies in her time and this was going to be her very last before her retirement. The village was already wearing its first heavy winter coat and a sharp north-easterly wind was making her journey wearisome.

Blue-lipped, she plodded through the narrow, uneven path when all of a sudden, the sun burst through a tiny gap between the heavy snow-laden clouds and transformed the sleeping valley for a moment or two into a morning shower of glistening crystal tears. It almost resembled a stage setting and was as if the curtains had opened with all the lights focused on the scenery ahead. The little houses nestled safely amongst its fir trees and sat snugly tucked within the sweeping hills. Above, like a monument, the snow-capped mountains responded with a scintillating sparkle and the mood was still and silent.

The Zenker family was already well known to Anna. In her time she had delivered the now expectant young mother, Elisabeth, as well as her many brothers, sisters and cousins.

It was quite natural in those days for young mothers to seek the solace and care of their mothers during their confinement, and with your father drafted by the German army to fight in Russia, it provided added reassurance. However, your arrival into the world was to prove no mean feat. The umbilical cord was firmly wrapped around your neck. I was instructed to call for the doctor as a matter of great urgency and, when the cheerful tingling bells of his horse-driven sleigh could be heard from afar, everybody breathed a sigh of relief. Finally, after a total of thirty-six hours' hard work, Anna's work was done.

She had delivered her thousandth baby and both mother and child were safe and well.

My birthplace, Katharinaberg

2. A WORLD AT WAR

At the time of the Munich Agreement in September 1938, Great Britain, France and Czechoslovakia wanted to prevent war at any cost. They perhaps somewhat naively, accepted Adolf Hitler's claim that the Sudeten grievances were justified. Since France did not want to face Hitler alone, it took the advice of Prime Minister Neville Chamberlain and the British government. A settlement was then reached, allowing the Nazi German annexation of Czechoslovakia's Sudetenland as part of a peace settlement to avoid a military confrontation with Hitler.

Soon afterwards, Hitler broke the agreement and marched his troops to Prague and occupied the whole of Czechoslovakia, assuming that nobody would intervene. He then invaded Poland as well and both Great Britain and France declared war on Germany. During the occupation of Czechoslovakia, the Czech people are said to have suffered terribly under the Nazis.

During World War II, Czechoslovakia ceased to exist and was divided into the Protectorate of Bohemia, Moravia and the newly declared Slovak Republic. After Germany surrendered in 1945, the area of Sudetenland was returned to Czechoslovakia and the German-speaking majority was expelled. Some were killed or died of starvation.

Nineteen forty-two, which was the year of my birth, was a year of unrest and great anxiety. It was the year when British and Indian troops were fighting the Japanese in Burma. After the bombing of Pearl Harbour and the fall of Singapore, the Japanese were left on the defensive.

With massive support, the Americans landed successfully on the Solomon Islands and were advancing inland against near-suicidal Japanese resistance. It was also the year when Gandhi named Pandit Nehru as his successor.

On the 20th January, officials learned of Gestapo leader Heydrich's 'final solution' to exterminate the 11 million Jews in Europe. Soon afterwards he was assassinated by Czech partisans. The Nazis began the deportation of Jews to Auschwitz concentration camp.

US planes bombed Tokyo. The Germans took Sevastopol after a nine-month siege and advanced on Stalingrad. In August, Gandhi and other Congress leaders were arrested. On 19th August Allied forces went ashore at Dieppe to gain experience of an amphibious attack against German coastal positions.

Brazil declared war on Germany and Italy and on 10th September the RAF dropped 100,000 bombs on Düsseldorf in Germany in under one hour.

I knew nothing of these realities of course and even when I was a little older the only indication I had was in being told that my father was a soldier and that he had to go away but would be back sometime. It didn't have any real significance. I had my mother and grandmother and I felt completely loved.

I had to wait until I was three years old to get a 'feeling of sadness' but even then I didn't know why. Events caused great concern for my mother and grandmother and for their friends and family but I was protected from their anxieties and allowed to enjoy the gift of innocent childhood.

Maya Kraus

3. RETURN TO TEPLITZ-SCHÖNAU

After a few weeks of rest my mother moved back to her home in Teplitz-Schönau. Teplitz was well known for its spas, and was relatively safe if you happened to be of German origin at that time. On her arrival at the train station my mother noticed a young mother who was sobbing uncontrollably. She was cowering in a corner with a small child. She approached her and asked her what the problem was. She told her that she was Czech and that the German officials had occupied her house and killed her husband but that she had managed to get away unharmed. My mother took the decision to engage her as her nanny. Her name was Olga. Since her little girl had blond hair and steel-blue eyes and looked very much like me, nobody took any notice.

My parents' house was very spacious and very soon afterwards the Gestapo occupied part of it as one of their quarters which placed my mother in a very difficult predicament by sheltering a Czech woman whose command of the German language was very poor. What to do? The consequences of discovery were very frightening. Eventually my mother came up with a brilliant plan to mislead the officers by making them believe that the nanny was mute. And it worked!

It was during this time that I experienced a painful incident when a uniformed German officer offered me some sweets. My mother, who was playing the piano, stopped abruptly, got up and, to my utter incomprehension, snatched them out of my hand and threw them out of the window. She then resumed playing the piano. This was unforgivable and an absolute deprivation as far as I was concerned and I sulked for hours. When pressing my mother many years later to explain the reason for her behaviour she told me that this man was a high-ranking leader of the Gestapo and refused any further explanation. Only much later did I come to realise how courageous my mother's action had been.

My father's house, Teplitz-Schönau

4. STRANGE ENCOUNTER

There was one other event at this time which remains firmly impregnated in my mind. One night whilst staying with my grandmother (as my mother and I often did) I heard the voice of a man talking to my grandmother. It was not a familiar voice but I had the strangest feeling that it was someone I should know. I crept out of bed and stood at the top of the stairs listening to the conversation.

My grandmother and the other person were speaking very quietly as if they were sharing a secret. I had no recollection of my grandfather, although I was aware of a photograph of him taken in happier times, but somehow I was absolutely convinced that he had come home. I ran down the stairs and saw an elderly, grey-haired man at the bottom of the stairs.

For a brief moment our eyes met. I called out, "Opa". The man turned round in a panic and rushed down a long dark corridor towards the toilet. I became hysterical. "I want to see my Opa," I screamed, running down the corridor and banging on the door of the toilet.

With some difficulty my grandmother restrained me and guided me back to my bedroom, calming me all the while and reassuring me that there was nothing to worry about. Later I heard the heavy front door being unlocked and then bolted up again. I waited anxiously until everything was quiet and then I tiptoed carefully down the stairs. The toilet door was wide open but there was no one inside! The front door was firmly locked. I decided to go back to my bedroom and from there I climbed out of the window and down an old pear tree that hugged the wall. Equipped with my 'schlummerl' (the remains of my very first duvet cover with its well-chewed four corners) I set off in search of my grandfather. When my mother discovered that I was missing she alerted the neighbours and soon the whole village was out looking for me with their lanterns.

Eventually at five o'clock in the morning, after seven hours of searching and calling, I was found fast asleep under the refuge of a big fir tree, my schlummerl clutched in my hands. I learned later that I had not been mistaken; it really was my grandfather whom I had seen that night. He was taking shelter from the pursuit of Czech partisans who were flushing out and seeking revenge on retreating German soldiers as the tide of the war turned against them.

If they had caught him he would almost certainly have been executed. Very sadly he was never seen again but the family learned through the Red Cross that he had died whilst a prisoner of war. The disturbing encounter of that night – the long dark corridor and haunted eyes of my grandfather – became a nightmare for many years to come.

5. EXPULSION

For centuries three million Germans had lived in the Czech lands which became part of Czechoslovakia after World War I. The main areas were situated around the borders with Germany in Sudetenland and, for the most part, they got along reasonably well with their Czech neighbours. When Czechoslovakia was liberated from the Nazis at the end of World War II the population of the country took its revenge – not just on the Nazis themselves but on all ethnic Germans, including women and children.

Across Czechoslovakia, thousands of Jews and some ethnic Germans – those brave enough to oppose the expulsion – were murdered, raped and tortured during this period. The expulsion was a plan carried out on the basis of a government programme hatched with the Allies towards the end of the war to expel without compensation three million Germans from the country. This act of ethnic cleansing was openly sanctioned by Churchill, Stalin and Truman and was carried out by the new president of Czechoslovakia: Eduard Benes. It was one of Europe's less honourable episodes and only recently has an official apology been made by the Czech government.

This programme had dramatic implications for my mother and her family. Once secure in the country she had been born in – in fact the only country she had known and felt herself to be part of – she now found herself in serious danger. My mother was only too aware of the hostility felt towards ethnic Germans and she had heard of terrible acts of retribution that were being played out by members of the Czech army and partisans. Her first move was to change roles with Olga (the false mute) and to pretend that she was employed by her as her 'Kinderfräulein' (nanny). Eventually, however, the situation became too dangerous for my mother to stay and, encouraged by my grandmother, she decided that the best option was to give up the house and to leave with me on one of the refugee trains used to deport expellees. Oma herself was hesitant to leave her parental home, a forester's house that her father had built, and she insisted on staying put, believing that she would be safe as my father had at one time served in the Czechoslovakian army. However, this proved to be false reasoning as will be explained later.

On arriving at the train station, all jewellery and anything of value, including my mother's fur coat, was removed by the Czech officials and after sorting through the suitcases – one per person was allowed – only a bundle of bare necessities remained. For my part I was still too young to comprehend the gravity of the situation. I was used to travelling about, particularly between my parents' house and my grandmother's and I accepted the situation as simply another outing, albeit a strange one that took place in the evening. Having said that, I must have absorbed something of the 'menace' because, even today when I watch a television programme or a film which shows a gun being pointed directly from the screen, I feel a frightening and disturbing coldness and I have to turn away.

I do remember that the train was unlike any train I was aware of. The carriage had a sliding door that could only be opened from the outside. No seats were provided except a few bales of straw. It was, in fact, a cattle wagon into which thirty or so people were boarded. It was crowded, smelly and stifling hot. My mother did her very best to comfort me by holding me close to her and singing songs to reassure me, but such was the tension and fear in the carriage that she was shouted at and told to be quiet. We endured many indeterminable hours of wearisome travelling with lots of stops and starts and creaking of chains from the couplings. There were no sanitation facilities or breaks in the journey.

The train finally stopped in Leinfelden, near Stuttgart in Germany, where three elderly couples, my mother and I were ordered to get out. The sudden exposure to daylight was like a sharp smack in the face and it took some time before strength returned to our limbs. Some makeshift barracks had been erected for shelter and we were directed to what was to be our new home until such time as the German authorities could arrange billeting within the local community.

There were no furnishings, just bales of straw for bedding and there was no food. Everyone had to fend for themselves. It was a desperately hard situation not helped by the animosity felt by the locals, many of whom were farmers who themselves were suffering hardship. The influx of newcomers was not wanted and we were considered gypsies and 'Reingeschmeckte' (vagabonds) and it happened many times during the first week or two, before new arrangements were put into force, that farmers set their dogs on unwelcome beggars seeking food. Despite the hardship we were the lucky ones. Many died whilst undergoing the ordeal of expulsion; some were deliberately executed, others were beaten with rifle butts or physically abused and many died of starvation. It is estimated that as many as two hundred and fifty thousand (some estimates are as high as four hundred thousand) non-Nazi ethnic Germans perished in an orgy of revenge.

Our first home in Germany in Leinfelden

6. GRANDMOTHER BERTA'S STORY

Despite my grandmother's reasoning, in May 1945 Czech soldiers moved to Katharinaberg and raided all the houses and took away all the animals (horses, cows, geese, goats and hens) and property, including furniture and carpets. With no livestock left, Oma made her way to East Germany. She loaded various items of bedding and a stove that she had managed to hide from the Czech pilferers onto a handcart and made her way over the mountains to the Czech border. Her progress was painfully laborious. All the borders were closed with barbed wire fences on both sides.

Once she arrived at the border, the remainder of her belongings was taken from her before she was allowed to cross the frontier into East Germany. There, she had to undergo the humiliating experience of being deloused by the Russians before proceeding further. Ethnic Germans were made to wear white armbands and a label on their chest marked 'N' and 'Katharinaberg'.

Eventually, she was given an identity card and received her permit to travel. She was then transported in a cattle wagon across the border which was occupied by the Russians and referred to as the Soviet Union (later on called DDR – Deutsche Demokratische Republik).

From there she was moved from one camp to another. Finally she was able to learn of our whereabouts and was reunited with us in Germany.

Berta, or Oma as I called her, like so many of the women during that time whose husbands were at war, was left to fend for herself and her children. With so many mouths to feed it meant that she had to attend single-handedly to all the everyday household chores as well as to the demands of a small farm: tending the cattle and chickens; churning the butter; planting potatoes and vegetables and doing the washing in the little stream nearby.

In the morning she would ring the cowbells, which was the waking-up signal for me to go to the cowshed – just three small steps down through a connecting door of the hallway of the house – in my long white cotton nightgown, to fill up my little red cup with warm fresh milk from the cows.

Every second day she would set off early in the morning to do the shopping in Katharinaberg and to gather firewood on the way home which she carried on her back, not an easy task in the mountains! This caused her back to gradually stoop forward until eventually she was bent forward by almost twenty degrees, which in turn affected her breathing. At night she would cough herself to sleep.

Later when she moved in with us in Leinfelden, she would spend the long winter months knitting socks with four needles in deadly concentration, wearing thick, brown-rimmed glasses. Oma always wore black clothes, some of which bore tiny pretty little white flowers, under which she wore numerous layers of white petticoats.

Every day, after lunch, she cut out a serial of a novel from the daily newspaper which she carefully added to the previous issues and bound it with string: it was her very own library! The rest of the paper was used as toilet paper, which I had to cut into squares then make a hole in the left-hand corner through which I threaded some string to finally hang up on a nail on a wall in our toilet.

Using the toilet was a most terrifying experience for me. Whenever it was a windy day, an enormous cold gust of wind came howling up the pipes straight onto my little bottom. This made me abandon my purpose and as a result I became very constipated.

I shared a bedroom with my Oma and at night I would watch her in fascination as she untied her hair which fell down in long, silky strands and she would brush it carefully. Then she would climb into bed and take out her rosary and move her hands from bead to bead, whispering some words that I didn't understand. By this time she had lost all her teeth.

One evening she carefully put her knitting needles away and took to her bed. She was very frail.

The whole family and the local priest were assembled at her bedside and after a final deep breath she closed her eyes and died peacefully. She had the air of a great Indian chief. I was nine years old.

7. GRANDMOTHER ANNA'S STORY

One morning at 5.30 a.m., after the end of the war, my grandmother on my father's side was woken up by a fearful noise outside the house. When my grandmother opened the door a mob of uniformed Czech soldiers stormed in, waving axes and huge batons and shouting, "alle Deutsche raus" ("All Germans Out").

My grandmother, her daughter Maria, who was 29 years of age and Emmi (her story is described later) were in the house. My grandmother and Emmi were ordered to get dressed and were told to wait in a downstairs room. Maria was forcefully returned to her bedroom and was joined by some of the men.

There was nothing my grandmother could do except plead for the release of her daughter. After some time the soldiers left the room pushing Maria ahead of them and ordered everyone out of the house. They were told to make their way to the local station. They were not allowed any possessions. When they reached the station they were instructed by Czech officials to board a waiting cattle wagon which then transported them out of the country.

Maria was unable to speak. She had been traumatised by the events that she had experienced earlier.

She couldn't even respond to the comfort that her mother attempted to give her. She simply sat for the whole journey staring out blankly.

When they arrived at the East German border they were ordered to disembark and from there they were told to make their own arrangements to Zinnwald, a nearby town. Eventually, they were offered a room above a bakery in return for doing cleaning. During this time the discovery of a small purse of money in Maria's coat pocket enabled the group to buy some food.

As the money was slowly running out, my grandmother asked the baker's wife if she could spare some butter and sausages, "At least for my children," she pleaded.

The answer was sharp and cold. "Trockenes Brot macht auch die Wangen rot!" ("Dry bread can also make the cheeks go red!")

One morning Maria found that her purse, which she had kept in the drawer in her bedside table in case of emergencies, was missing. My grandmother, unwisely as it happened, mentioned this to the baker's family who reacted violently and literally threw them out of the house shouting after them "Undankbares Volk!" ("Ungrateful riff-raff!")

Once again they made their way to the station where they boarded a train to Dresden in the hope of seeking help from relatives. On arrival my grandmother couldn't get her bearings. There were no familiar and distinctive landmarks. The whole city had been reduced to rubble. In the midst of this devastation a piece of good fortune presented itself. Two young girls in a state of great happiness introduced themselves to the wandering group. It was a strange and almost surreal sight that there should exist any notion of joy in a setting of such devastation and misery. It turned out that they wanted to share the news that both their fiancés were alive and would be returning home shortly.

The girls arranged for my grandmother and the girls to stay at one of their homes until they could sort themselves out. It was an act of great kindness. Later they helped my grandmother and the children to get in touch with the US Army who arranged for them to travel to Hanau, in Franken, Germany, where accommodation was provided for the small family and where they settled for a number of years.

Maria, who was a renowned artist and had exhibited her work in a prestigious art gallery in Teplitz prior to these tragic events, sadly was never able to realise her full potential. Her trauma weighed heavily upon her and in the end she lacked the will to leave her bed and she simply wasted away.

A year later, my parents found a room near us for my grandmother and Emmi. When Emmi was 16 years old she began an apprenticeship in tailoring, under the tutelage of my father. Eventually, she passed the qualification of master tailor for gentlemen and ladies! We were all so very proud of her.

8. NEW LIFE IN LEINFELDEN

Eventually things improved. After a few weeks of hardship after our arrival in Leinfelden, my mother was offered a room in the house of a local tailor, which had become vacant when his son was killed during the war. In return for this hospitality, my mother worked as a seamstress and helped him in his business.

During my mother's working hours, I remained in the care of my grandmother but I had a lot of freedom to play with friends. One summer's day, whilst playing outside I heard a terrifying rumbling sound coming from afar. It felt as if the ground beneath me was vibrating fiercely. What was it? Could it be an earthquake? I was very worried and thought the world was coming to an end. The noise got louder and louder and the ground shook violently and suddenly there appeared a column of huge American tanks like giant monsters moving slowly in file towards where I was playing. They were stationed nearby in Böblingen and were out on one of their manoeuvres. The convoy of tanks and vehicles seemed never-ending.

Amidst the deafening noises of the tanks' engines, the children of the village swarmed around and shouted slogans to the American soldiers, which seemed to amuse them and prompted them to throw chewing gum to the barefoot children who scrambled to retrieve it.

I joined in, merrily copying the words of the slogans and the soldiers just laughed. It was only later, during English tuition at school, that I discovered the dubious content of their meanings and felt both embarrassed and ashamed.

It so happened that on one of these occasions I found myself as the only one left on the wrong side of the road. No chewing gum! At that moment, little Edi appeared and with a huge smile from his freckled face rummaged around in one of the bulging pockets of his trousers, which seemed at least three sizes too big, to retrieve some precious gum. Talk about instant bonding. He was a friend for life and I followed him home.

The Town Hall of Leinfelden
by Walter Schimpf

9. THE ROSEWIRT FAMILY

Edi was the youngest of twelve children. His parents owned the biggest house in Leinfelden and were the publicans of 'Gasthaus Rose', a pub with never-ending corridors, stairways and rooms. There was also a slaughterhouse and a butcher's shop annexed to it. Edi's mother Frau Rosewirt, received me affectionately with open arms.

She was huge and I always enjoyed soaking into the enormous mass of her embrace when she welcomed me although I could never understand why she was always sobbing and why she would hand out a slap to any one of her children if they happened to venture unwisely within her reach. I later discovered that she was treated very badly by her husband who became violent when he was drunk, which was often.

The Rosewirts owned one of the biggest Kachelofens (a tiled heating stove) imaginable. So big in fact that Edi's grandfather would often be seen sitting on top, propped up under his duvet smoking a pipe. How he managed to climb up there I couldn't work out. I was invited to visit the pub whenever I wanted and I looked forward to it especially as Edi, my hero, was never far away!

Edi always had to wear clothes handed down from his bigger brothers. His shorts went below his knees and he had to hold them up with braces. From time to time he would pull his braces up to his head and then let them go quickly so that they fired back onto his shoulders with a loud smacking noise. Then he would laugh and laugh.

Whenever he had a runny nose he would wipe it with his sleeve and some of the snot remained on his cheeks for days. I never saw him with a clean face yet the mischievous sparkle in his bright blue eyes captivated me.

The Rosewirt family, having grown fond of me, offered lodgings to my mother. They comprised a large combined living room and bedroom and there was a kitchen, situated at the end of a long, dark corridor which always posed a menace to me, in case there were ghosts. Although my grandmother, Oma Berta, remained in a separate room in the village for the first few years, she spent her whole day with us attending to all the washing and ironing, mending of stockings, knitting and cooking. The cooking was mainly of Czech and Austrian origin.

The hardship suffered during two world wars became of immense value once again. By adding only basic seasonal ingredients, the culinary delights she managed to conjure from only flour, potato or semolina was never-ending.

She would produce dumplings with fillings of fried bread, or simply made with flour and yeast, over which we poured delicious vanilla custard. My favourite dish was plum dumplings, filled with Mirabellen (yellow plums).

We sprinkled a mixture of sugar and cinnamon over the dumplings, added some hot milk and a little melted butter. Everyone was always so hungry and appreciative. She was also skilled in making my father's shirts look as good as new, by turning the freighted collar and cuffs inside out. Whenever one of our pullovers displayed yawning big holes, she would unravel the wool and reknit it into an almost new sweater.

Maya Kraus

10. HAPPY DAYS

During the months of late spring and early autumn I enjoyed the outdoors. School finished at twelve o'clock and as soon as the church bells rang my faithful friend Senta, a German shepherd dog who belonged to the butcher's shop, would be waiting outside the makeshift school barracks to greet me.

It was a wonder to me how Senta could tell the time, since she arrived most days seconds before the striking of the church bells. She was very loyal and we were good friends although I couldn't understand why she wouldn't allow me to share her kennel.

I so wanted Senta to be my very own dog! I came up with a sudden inspiration: I knocked at the door of the Butcher's couple, who had a room on the same corridor as us, opposite our kitchen. When Frau Wengel answered the door, I asked her whether I could exchange Senta with my Granny, Oma. She looked at me with her usual stern face and I quickly added: 'My Oma can sow and cook.'

Instead of a reply, Frau Wengel closed the door on me. A few days later my mother told me that Oma was very upset when she found out that I wanted to exchange her for a dog. I couldn't understand this and I replied: 'But I can see her every day!'

Later on, when I started school, all the pupils had to share one room in a makeshift hut. The younger ones sat at the front and the older children at the back. I very seldom saw Edi attending. Whenever he tried to sneak into the classroom, the teacher would notice him immediately and called him to the front desk. He then got beaten severely with a cane for not attending school and not doing his homework. When he was asked why he missed many days of school, he would reply that he had to work for his father. The truth was that he was in the forest building a tree house for us to play in. The girls didn't get the cane, instead the teacher would pull hard on their plaits or ponytails until they cried. I wore a ponytail and, after having received the same treatment for chatting in class, I decided to cut off my ponytail with my father's big scissors. The result was not what I expected – my hair was a complete mess and my mother was furious.

With school over for the day it was home for lunch and then to play, climbing trees, playing hide-and-seek in the forest or running around with an old pram wheel which Edi and I converted into a hoop and hit it with a stick. The greatest fun was sneaking into people's gardens and helping ourselves to the early cherries, apples and pears.

We had to watch out for the Feldpolizei (Field Police) who were employed to keep an eye out for 'scrumpers'. On one occasion I was busy harvesting some cherries in a tree when the call came from Edi to "climb down quickly" because a man in a green uniform was approaching. We ran home as fast as our little legs would carry us, taking care not to drop our illicit bounty which we held securely in our jumpers.

We set eyes on the best apple tree in the village with the biggest and the reddest apples we had ever seen. Whenever we attempted to climb over the fence an old man appeared from nowhere and chased us away waving a big garden rake. One day Edi came to collect me because he had seen the old man on his way to the grocer's shop.

This was our moment but on our arrival at the garden and to our dismay, we discovered that all the apples had gone except for three enormous specimens at the very top of the tree. Edi found some wire and for revenge he climbed up the tree and fixed the apples onto the branches. During this operation one of the apples fell down and I put it into my apron pocket to share later on. It was our reward. For a number of days we watched, with malicious joy, the old man trying to retrieve the remaining two apples with a large pole but to no avail. The apples stayed resolutely fixed to the tree.

In the early autumn Edi and I would sneak to nearby fields where Sauerkraut (cabbages) stood proudly upright like soldiers, two feet tall, as far as the eye could see.

We broke off the tips and feasted on the crunchy, juicy leaves which were very tasty at the time but filled us with wind which we expelled with glee.

One day Edi had a great idea. He found a penny on the road and was certain that if he placed it on the railway line the train would flatten and enlarge it and we could buy thousands of sweets. Edi set up the penny and we waited with great anticipation for the jolly whistle to herald the approach of the train. We stood and watched the train thunder by and then moved in eagerly to see if the plan had worked. Great joy, the penny was flattened to three times its original size. We skipped to the grocer's shop to collect our reward but the shopkeeper, Herr Kästner, shook his head and told us that the flattened coin was no longer worth its original penny.

In early summer we were invaded by Maikäfer beetles (cockchafers). They were about one inch long and had beautiful white zigzag markings on either side of their brown bodies. The boys would creep up on the girls and push them down their backs, causing great squeals of pleasurable horror. We used to collect the beetles and put them in small boxes with a supply of leaves from lilac trees for food. One day a helicopter came and sprayed our forest to combat these beetles. It produced an alarming sight as they dropped out of the trees in a never-ending shower and this is the last we ever saw them.

One of our early-morning duties was to collect the milk from the local dairy farm using metal cans with handles. On the way back Edi and I held a competition as to how many times we could swing the cans without losing any milk. This involved a great deal of skill as the cans were very heavy but the most difficult part was controlling the swing when bringing it to stop. One day our cans collided in full swing and we lost all the milk. We had quite a lot of explaining to do.

Whenever opportunity presented itself and at great risk I would help Edi untie the sacks of little lambs stacked outside the slaughterhouse awaiting their fate and then shoo them away. Then we would run and hide in the barn, climbing onto a raised shelf and pulling up the heavy ladder behind us.

We climbed trees and made fairy castles in the forest, which we covered with patches of moss and I constructed animal hospitals for wounded birds and beetles. Edi helped to supply patients by cutting up worms. Unfortunately nothing could be done for the poor old cockerel that I witnessed flying madly around the butcher's yard without a head!

On rainy days, Edi and I enjoyed sliding down the steep banisters (which was not allowed) or I would join with the Rosewirt children in the pub, which afforded a good view of the road outside. We challenged each other who could build the tallest towers with brewery beermats. From here we would spot horse droppings (Rossbollen) and we would rush out to collect the spoils in little buckets which would then be used as fertiliser for the allotment. I also got to know the locals who came into the pub to drink.

When the language became 'ripe' all the children were ordered to leave the bar area. We would seek refuge in the big barn where Liane would find the greatest delight in frightening us with horror stories. Liane, at the time, was the only daughter of the Rosewirts but soon afterwards three more girls were born in close succession.

We just sat there transfixed by the horror stories, starry-eyed and open-mouthed and in my case, it caused me many troubled nights of sleep for months to come.

One of the worst nightmares I experienced was hearing a terrifying sharp hissing sound above me and coming closer towards me in slow motion. I desperately sought refuge under a table waiting anxiously for a bomb to explode. At that moment, I usually woke up with my heart pounding. This same deeply distressing dream carried on for many years. I cannot say for certain but it seems reasonable to assume that the trauma lay deep within my subconscious and the nightmare was the manifestation of a wartime experience.

Edi and me at play

Maya Kraus

11. STRANGE SIGHTS

There was a village idiot who was really harmless and we enjoyed teasing him because when he became excited he would make barking noises at us.

We were warned about mad dogs and on one occasion I saw a dog with foam on its mouth. It was wavering from one side of the road to the other and coming towards me. I ran away as fast as I could.

From time to time we saw a chimney sweep carrying various long brushes over his shoulder. His black face, contrasting with the whites of his eyes, spooked us. Edi told me that he was a creature from another land and we always made sure that there was plenty of distance between us in case we were kidnapped.

Whenever we saw the tall figure of the railway sleeper man we would follow him at a distance, copying his long, measured steps. His job was to walk along the railway lines to check the nuts and bolts and he walked with such assured strides that sometimes we could not keep up with him and lost our footing on the sleepers.

The shrill ringing of a bell brought us all running excitedly to see who had arrived in the village. Sometimes it was the rag-and-bone man, or a knife grinder who sharpened the scissors of my father. The most exciting arrival was the cider man. He pulled a large barrel of cider on his handcart and a smaller barrel containing delicious apple juice and I was only allowed to fill my little jug but it tasted like heaven!

The only means of getting about was by foot or catching the Strassenbahn (tram) that went every hour to Stuttgart. So it could happen, when I was older, that on many occasions I would set off to visit a distant friend and after walking for over an hour I would perhaps discover that she was not at home and had to return. I did manage to learn to ride a bike but as it was a bike belonging to Herr Rosewirt I had to negotiate my leg under the crossbar and through the frame to reach the outer pedal. As you can imagine, this made steering very difficult and progress was somewhat erratic.

Edi was particularly good at riding the bike, and being led by his older brothers who showed off by steering with their bare feet, he developed the skill of riding without hands on the handlebars. It was an impressive show until one day the bike took a perverse course that led him to steer straight into a beer lorry where he lost a front tooth and gained, thereafter, a lisp.

It was all play and adventures – rose-tinted memories!

12. TRAGEDIES

There were some real tragedies at this time, which I was old enough to appreciate.

One day when I looked out of our window, I saw two policemen approaching the Pub. Being curious, I went downstairs and saw the policemen talking to Frau Rosewirt. I could sense that something terrible had happened and I could see that Edi's mother's face was white. She had just learned that one of her sons, Bernd, had died in a tragic accident. Bernd, who was eighteen years old, was riding his motorbike and took a corner too fast and ended up impaled on a tree. Edi, who was a passenger, was thrown into a hedge. Edi's face was bleeding and his legs were full of scratches. One of the policemen asked Edi what had happened. He said that all he could remember was that Bernd's brain was dripping down a tree trunk. Frau Rosewirt, on hearing this, gave Edi a severe smack on his cheek which sent him flying all the way across the room.

On another occasion I was about to descend the stairs when I heard a lot of shouting and screaming from the kitchen below me. I hid behind the banister where I had a clear view into the kitchen. I watched with absolute horror as Edi's older brother attacked the butcher's wife with a kitchen knife. The butcher tried to stop him and in doing so was stabbed to death.

Heinz was later arrested and sent to prison. I have never shared this terrifying incident with anyone up to this day.

Another event which I remember was the ringing of the church bells. Normally they rang to celebrate a wedding or a call-out to the volunteer firemen. On this occasion it was for the latter. There was huge excitement from the villagers who gathered to witness the burning down of a barn which belonged to a local farmer.

The villagers were very concerned believing that the farmer was still inside the barn. Eventually the fire was put out and there was little left of the barn. Following an investigation it was revealed that the farmer had in fact committed suicide. That morning he had withdrawn all his money from the bank and then set fire to the barn and had hanged himself from one of the rafters. The money was later discovered still charred in his pockets.

And then there was the day when a young woman whom I admired for her beauty and whose graceful walk I tried to imitate was found dead in the forest. The murderer turned out to be the policeman's son who lived two houses away from us. He was brought to justice because his father found a glove in her mouth that matched that given by him to his son as a Christmas present. Edi took me to the fateful spot where we stood in silence and stared and stared. And we didn't even know her name!

13. MY NEW 'PAPA'

With so many friends to play with and so many houses to visit I suddenly woke up to a realisation – I had no father! I decided instantly to do something about it. I had to have a father and he had to be handsome and live in a big house. I decided that the father of a little boy (who, for some strange reason we could not understand always ran back into his house whenever we invited him to play with us) was perfect. Anxiously, I knocked at his door one day and asked him whether he would like to be my 'Neuer Papa'.

He laughed gently and took me by the hand and led me into his huge drawing room where he placed me on his lap and agreed to my request. And so it was and all was well. Or so I thought.

On a subsequent visit he invited me to come into his living room where he sat me down on his knees and bounced me up and down in a playful game called 'Hoppe Reiter'. Suddenly he stopped and asked me to come back the next day. After collecting a loaf of bread for my family I called in to see him as arranged. When I entered his living room he locked the door and the curtains were drawn.

I asked him why and he answered: "Because it is our secret," and added, "before we play 'Hoppe Reiter' you need to take off your underpants.

Who knows where you have been and I am wearing my new trousers. I have also bought a big bar of chocolate for you."

Chocolate – what a wonderful treat! I looked at his trousers which seemed quite old and crumpled up to me. Then he sat me on his knees and started to bounce me up and down. At first it was quite good fun until he started to fumble about and my little bottom started to hurt. I asked him to stop.

He put me back on the floor and pointed to his trouser area. "This is your little friend and it wants to play with you."

I felt paralysed at what I saw. Flashes of memories reminded me of a game I played with Edi called 'Dead Man'. One of us used to pretend to be a tiger or a lion and if we caught the other one, we had to lie down and pretend to be dead.

One day Edi told me that he was a snake. "They don't have legs but they do have a tongue as long as my arm and if I catch you I must lick you with my tongue and you will be dead."

What I saw was a big snake peeping out of my 'new papa's' trousers.

Journey of a Healer

I screamed and struggled and managed to wriggle free and ran to the door, kicking at it with my feet and shouting, "Snake, snake, open the door!"

Eventually he unlocked it and said that I was a very naughty girl and I would only get the chocolate when I come back. I ran away, without picking up my pants and the loaf of bread. I never went back. When I returned home my mother and grandmother were surprised to see me empty-handed and asked, "Where is our bread?"

I lied and told her that a giant dog had jumped up at me and stolen the bread. This meant that we had no bread for the day which was a serious deprivation because at that time we lived off rations and could only claim one loaf of bread per family every second day.

From then on, I always crossed the road to avoid my 'new papa's' house. One day I saw a farmer's daughter, about five years older than me, sitting on the steps of his house, unwrapping a large bar of chocolate. I wanted to warn her about the danger she was in and ventured out to the middle of the road. When I called out to her she stuck her tongue out at me in a very unpleasant manner and then carried on eating.

Maya Kraus

14. MY TRUE FATHER

One day soon after this encounter with my 'new papa', I heard my mother's heart-warming laughter ringing out from the window of our living room. I rushed up the stairs and opened the door. I saw a tall, slim man hugging my mother. He turned round and, although I had never met him before, when I looked into his eyes I knew with absolute certainty that he was my father, Alois.

He was one of the few who had made it back from the Russian front and survived as a prisoner of war in France. My mother was smiling and looked radiantly happy and encouraged me to say hello. We shook hands formally and I bent my knees for a curtsey the way I had been taught. Then I burst out: "I don't like to play 'Hoppe Reiter'." My father looked quite puzzled and turned to my mother who was equally mystified. He ensured me that this was all right with him. Then I turned round, relieved, and rushed out of the room to play.

Alois was the eldest son of five children. His mother came from a long line of teachers and, when she received the tragic news that her husband had been killed in the war and food became desperately scarce, she decided to send Alois, who was bright and talented, to an orphanage in Salzburg – a Franciscan convent which had the reputation for high educational standards. Life was extremely hard however, and the rules were very strict. Hunger was a constant discomfort, so much so that one night, together with two friends, he climbed out of a bedroom window to sneak into a pigsty to scrape off the remains of turnips. Of course it was impossible to hide the evidence of these nightly escapades because their muddy nightgowns gave them away. As a punishment he and his two friends were made to scrub clean the cloister, which was covered with ice and snow at that time, every morning before breakfast, for several weeks and without the protection of gloves.

After his final school year at the convent was over his mother could not afford to finance any further studies as well as support his brothers and sisters and he was sent to become an apprentice to a tailor in his hometown of Teplitz. He had always had a fascination for engineering and hated every moment of this enforcement and on one occasion he tried to escape to Austria to ask an uncle for help, only to be sent back to continue his apprenticeship. This is how he became a tailor.

Later in life he married but his happiness was short-lived. Visiting the maternity hospice, a proud and excited father, carrying a pot of pink geraniums, he opened the door to his wife's room and found her lying dead in a pool of blood holding a little sleeping baby in her lifeless arms. The baby, a daughter, was named Emmi after her mother Emilia.

When my mother and Alois married, Emmi was accepted and loved by my mother as her own. One day, however, when Emmi was five years old she ran crying distraughtly to her grandmother who lived nearby, and refused to return home. What was the matter? It was discovered later that a woman in the village had decided that Alois was the perfect match for her eldest daughter, who had still to find a suitor, and on being thwarted had spitefully sought out Emmi and told her that she was not living with her real mother.

Emmi remained with her grandmother from then on and although she continued to be part of our family, sadly the fracture with my mother never healed. There were to be other sad events in my father's life. His brother was killed in the war and his favourite sister Hedwig, a matron in a Teplitz hospital, contracted typhoid and died.

Maya Kraus

15. MY FATHER'S ARMY CAREER

As a young man, Alois Altrichter served some time with the Czechoslovakian army. However, when Germany invaded Czechoslovakia he was conscripted to the German army and sent to fight on the Russian front where he was captured and held in a prisoner of war camp. In circumstances that were never made clear – and maybe for very good reason – he managed to escape from the prison and made his way back to Czechoslovakia. Suffice it to say that the escape involved a young woman, a covered cart and a great deal of courage on both their parts. It had all the ingredients of a good wartime thriller except, of course, this was not fiction.

Once back in Czechoslovakia he regrouped with the German army and, in July 1943, he was moved to Northern Germany to assist in the artillery defence of the town of Hamburg. His battalion arrived too late. When they finally reached the town they witnessed a succession of nightly raids by many hundreds of British aircraft sending white phosphorus bombs over the city. Many tens of thousands of inhabitants literally melted alive.

This was cruel irony since it was in Hamburg that the scientist Hennig Brand, an alchemist about 250 years before, had researched the effectiveness of the element phosphorus.

He found that in combination with some other liquid a small fire could be created in a glass and he used this discovery as an amusing and harmless spectacle. Years later, in 1819, his innovation was put to practical use and phosphorus lamps were made. What happened afterwards became a brutal and shocking history.

After Hamburg Alois was sent to fight in France where once again he was captured, this time by the French forces. However, good fortune was to play its part once again – not by any intriguing circumstances like his previous escape but by the call of nature. The prisoner of war camp occupied a large field and the prisoners were housed in tents, each holding several prisoners. Late one evening Alois left the tent to go to the toilet which was situated a little way off.

Whilst engaged he could hear the noise of some French soldiers, who appeared the worse for drink, and the sound of gunfire. When he returned to his tent he discovered that one of his fellow comrades had been killed by a stray bullet. From the position of the unfortunate victim it was obvious that, had Alois stayed in the tent, the bullet would have hit him first.

This is the only wartime story my father shared with me even though I tried to get him to tell me more. At such times he cut me short with a curt "You don't understand!"

When the war ended and after spending nine months recuperating in a Lazaret (war hospital), the Red Cross arranged for Alois to be repatriated to Germany and reunited with his family in Leinfelden. He had experienced the horrors of man's inhumanity to man and endured severe hardships but he had survived where many had not. He was thirty-five years old.

My father, as I knew him, was a quiet man not given to social exuberance but he was a good listener and indicated his interest with a gentle smile or an acknowledging nod of the head. He seemed to be in a 'contained bubble of isolation'. There were occasions when he displayed more engagement.

In Czechoslovakia he sang in the church choir (where he met my mother) and where he was also a member of the Teplitz Opera choir. In Leinfelden he and my mother joined the local choral society. When at work tailoring, he would listen to operas and operettas or to songs by famous soloists, such as Elisabeth Schwarzkopf. Sometimes he would join in with the famous tenor, Richard Tauber, although he found it challenging to reach the high notes.

I loved my father very much and was very close to him. I would sit for hours watching him at work and was fascinated by his hands working deftly over the material.

I enjoyed listening to the rhythm of the clicking scissors and humming of the sewing machine which I found very comforting and it would often send me to sleep.

Young as I was, I sensed the grief and sadness within my father and his sorrows became my shadow.

In the 1950s my father suffered a serious setback in his work. He was a casualty of the mass production era. One could buy suits off the peg at C&A in Stuttgart for half the price of a bespoke suit. Gradually, he found himself doing more and more alteration work but eventually even this dried up and, having no other qualifications, he accepted employment in the postal department of the Allianz Insurance Company as a means of financial survival. A few years later he suffered a stroke which kept him housebound and unable to speak for seven years. He died peacefully in his sleep, taking all his secrets with him.

At the funeral my mother arranged for a brass band to play from a position on the side of a hill overlooking the graveside. As soon as I heard the trumpet fanfare I remembered my father telling me how much he enjoyed learning the trumpet that had been given to him by a teacher with whom he formed a deep friendship and came to regard as the father figure he had never had.

Unfortunately, my father developed verdigris on his lips caused by a mouthpiece made of inferior brass and he had to abandon playing the trumpet.

It struck me as very poignant at this time and I was overcome with emotion and shed bitter tears, not only for the loss of my father, but for the fact that he was denied realising his full potential which, I felt, he so dearly deserved. I promised myself then, whenever possible, to live out some of his unlived life.

All his life he seemed to live within a constraining 'square'. Whenever an opportunity presented itself for something rewarding, circumstances forced him back into the square. And so he bravely soldiered on and brave he was; amongst his possessions I discovered an iron cross that he had been awarded for bravery during the Second World War.

Maya Kraus

16. THE ALLOTMENT

My parents found an allotment where they spent all of Saturday and Sunday afternoon working until late. Potato beetles had to be collected and exterminated and this was my job which I achieved by jumping on them. Their crackling sound was most satisfying. On many occasions when my parents were too busy tailoring to attend to the allotment I would go with my grandmother. When, after a time, the walk became too challenging for her I would sit her in a homemade rack-wagon and pull her behind me. We sang songs from our homeland with all our hearts, causing the rabbits to scuttle to safety in the high-banked lanes.

When we were thirsty my grandmother would point out some plants to chew. She showed me how to extract oils from beechnuts and how to make flour from discarded wheat once the harvest was over. This was how I came to gain knowledge about the medicinal properties of plants which has served me all through my life and work ever since.

Such was my grandmother's intimate knowledge of the remedial benefits of nature that she soon established herself as something of a healer and people from all around the neighbourhood would visit her for treatment.

Maya Kraus

17. ILLNESS AND CONVALESCING

Between the ages of five and nine years old I had to pass my time during most of the winter or early spring in bed or away from my family. Every year I was sent, for many weeks at a time, to various children's sanatoriums in the Black Forest in Germany where I was treated for pleurisy, pneumonia and even tuberculosis.

Since the Black Forest was occupied at that time by the French army, no visitors were allowed. Only the Red Cross had access to children in hospitals or convalescence homes. I knew that I had a loving home to go back to and regarded my illness as a nuisance but something that would pass. All I had to do was to be patient and all would be well. I was a survivor!

Even so it was a dull existence since I possessed only a few books which I read and reread. I studied yellow flypaper dangling from the base of the ceiling light, clotted with flies and bluebottles. Sometimes I got so bored that I became skilful at capturing the flies that flew around in concentric circles and finally settled on my duvet only to be captured and imprisoned in my matchbox. When there was nothing else to do I would watch with amazement at flies walking upside down on the ceiling, rubbing their legs. Curiosity led me to wonder how they would fly without wings.

There was only one way to find out and my experiments concluded that they spin round in circles. It didn't occur to me that I may have inflicted suffering during these experiments.

At other times I would make up stories – always with happy endings. Or I would spend hours observing the layered clouds in the sky interpreting the formations as lions, dogs, fluffy cats, rabbits and majestic mountains harbouring sleepy giants with one eye. One particular giant image haunted me many times during my feverish nights. He would look down at me from the ceiling, brandishing an enormous butcher's knife!

Often I had no appetite which caused some concern but Edi, my loyal friend, came up with a good idea, which he kept secret from me at that time. He asked my Oma to make some of her wholesome chicken soup which he then gave to his mother, Frau Rosewirt, to serve it up to me in one of her own soup bowls. She pretended that she had cooked the soup herself. I didn't wish to appear ungrateful, so I ate it all up. It was delicious. So much better than Oma's soup! This was a procedure my parents had to play every lunch time.

During one of these hospital stays I made friends with a girl named Marianne. She was very beautiful with wide blue-green eyes and was five years my senior.

We shared the same bed and I would listen with awe to the tales of the many adventures she and her grandfather had experienced escaping from wolves in the Hessian hills.

Every afternoon after spending two long hours lying outside under a covered but open terrace, which did not always provide shelter from the icy wind and heavy snowfalls, we had to put on coats, hats and scarves and take a walk in the forest. One day when I was not feeling well I lagged behind and became lost. I had no sense of where I was and eventually I sat down by a tree feeling very cold and tired.

After some time and with the light fading, it was Marianne who found me and led me back to safety. She showed me great kindness. When I suffered from nightmares she would prop her pillow under my head and sing soothingly to me. Sometimes a nursing sister would notice that I had two pillows and would snatch it away from under me and once again the spectre of the giant with his knife and one eye would appear on the ceiling.

One night Marianne was missing. Where could she be?

Carefully, I crept out of bed to search for her. My instinct led me down a dimly lit corridor to a little box room. It was an area strictly forbidden to us children.

Reaching the box room, I stood on my toes and opened a tiny sliding window. There she was, my beautiful Marianne lying serenely on a bed.

The following night I crept down the corridor again and opened the sliding window to find that the bed was empty and that the blankets had been folded neatly and placed at one end.

Some weeks later I woke up and saw eyes staring at me from a small opening in a window, which was shut abruptly as soon as our eyes met. I was completely disorientated. Where was I? Am I dreaming?

Then I realised with alarm that I was in the same little box room where I had seen my beloved friend, Marianne, for the last time. I didn't want to die and I resolved to get out of there at all costs. I asked God to forgive me for all the naughty games I had played and promised to be good for ever. After three days of deep sleep my fever receded and I was allowed to rejoin the other children. I was on my way to recovery and after a total of three months without having been able to see my parents I was allowed to return home.

18. THE CIRCUS HAS COME TO TOWN

I must have been about six years old when, one day, the air around our village buzzed with excitement. Metal trumpet sounds and drumming noises announced the arrival of a travelling circus. I was allowed to visit its first performance.

I saw bareback riders doing acrobatics on horses. Then a big drum roll announced the highlight of the evening. I watched with awe as two trapeze artists climbed up two small steep ladders, opposite each other, to the very top of the tent, almost reaching the sky. They commenced by swinging towards each other to warm up and then, all of a sudden one of the girls let go of the swing and caught the arms of her partner in mid air. They continued performing amazing stunts and daring somersaults, all flying silently and gracefully in the air.

I decided that this was what I really, really wanted to do when I was big enough. When the circus came to the end of its stay and was preparing to move on I approached one of the clowns and begged him to let me come with them because I wanted to learn to fly the trapeze. He introduced me to a tall man with big black eyes, a huge moustache and big biceps.

He asked me: "Where is your mother?" and I lied. "She is away," I told him. "And your father?" I told him that he was lost in the war. Another lie.

He took me to one of the caravans and placed me in the care of a woman who I think must have been his wife. A few hours later we were on the move.

We only got as far as the next village, when my father suddenly arrived on his Lambretta. Since I hadn't returned for the evening meal and didn't turn up by seven o'clock, my father asked Edi if he knew where I was but he said that he had not seen me. Then he asked my sister who remembered seeing me hanging around the 'gypsies' all day.

My flight of fancy was up. This put an end to my dream of flying the trapeze although another opportunity was to present itself many years later.

19. MY MOTHER

My mother, Elisabeth, was one of five children and very beautiful with something of an aristocratic bearing. My appreciation of this became more obvious when I was able to read a beautifully presented book given to my mother by a distinguished historian who had explored the von Zenger aristocracy. This book contained well-researched documentation and fine drawings of its history, including many castles the family owned, dating back to 1009. Less attractive, perhaps, was the appellation of the 'Robber Barons' attributed to them during the Middle Ages.

My mother was petite, dark-haired and always wore bright red lipstick. She had a soprano voice that I can only describe as that of a charming Viennese quality. She used to sing with the opera in Teplitz and, when she wasn't too tired, she would sing happy little arias from Lehár to me which I adored. I was always so proud to be seen with my parents on the way to church. My father, so handsome and polite, always wearing a hat, and my mother so elegantly dressed in her Sunday costume, made by my father, which fitted smoothly around her small waist, complete with hat and matching gloves and shiny shoes.

Before my mother met my father, she found employment in Teplitz at the famous local spa, where people took their waters.

An elderly aunt of hers offered her free accommodation in her spacious mansion. She had a day-care nurse and she needed someone to take care of her at night. So it happened that, on many occasions, and after a long day's work, her aunt would ring her bell to summon my mother up to her bedroom, often during the middle of the night, to give her a massage or a drink. When the aunt learned that Elisabeth was going to get married, she got very excited and decided to plan a great wedding. When my mother introduced Alois to her she was impressed by his politeness, gallantry and good looks. Later she took her niece to a tailor to measure her for an exquisite bridal dress.

Then the aunt discovered that her niece was going to be married to a tailor. In disgust the aunt made it very clear that she would disinherit her should she marry below her social station and that there would be no wedding celebration taking place in her house! When she died, Elisabeth was not included in her will.

Unlike my father, my mother was very 'outward' in nature and was always very positive. Despite all that had happened to her she never lost the hope that things would turn out well in the end. She didn't dwell on the past or display regret for the loss of her house and homeland. Her optimism and character was a great source of strength during the difficult times.

20. FAMILY LIFE

With the return of my father new house rules had to be respected. Mealtimes were sacred. This meant that we had to be seated at the table at twelve noon and six o'clock sharp. After a prayer was said, everybody had to remain silent. Since my parents got up at dawn and worked late into the night it was important to respect their space. Whilst eating, the only sound that was accepted was the clutter of cutlery and its scraping against the china. Being a lively child I found this enforced silence very difficult and a bit ridiculous, and this would result in my making a self-conscious chuckle which brought frowns of disapproval from my parents. I couldn't wait to leave the table to make for the kitchen where I could be myself.

We were encouraged to be polite and say "Guten Tag" when greeting people in the street, unless they were strangers. The men would lift their hats respectfully to my mother or only touch the rim lightly if they were less acquainted. Every time we met Herr Adler he would bend down and squeeze my cheek firmly and say, "Hallo, Maidie".

This made my lips move to my ears and I was horrified in case they stayed there and I ran home as fast as I could to check in the mirror.

I was also not allowed to look back when anybody passed my way. It was a compulsion and I could never resist the temptation to turn around. I was instructed always to stay within earshot of the church bells, always to appear with clean aprons at the dinner table and never to show my knickers! Here I showed great ingenuity (and a great deal more) by simply taking my dress and apron off when playing outside and hanging them over a branch of a tree.

So I learned from an early age to observe and to listen with interest, to be discreet and never to interrupt when I wasn't spoken to. It wasn't easy. I had an abundance of imagination and energy and was easily impressionable and curious. Whenever I expressed an unreasonable demand for some material possession my mother would simply say: "Contentment lasts". It was a strict but loving childhood and the emphasis on good manners and respect for others prepared me well for my personal and professional life.

21. SCHAFFE, SCHAFFE, HÄUSLE BAUA AND STERBA

This means "work, work, build your house and die" – a well-known motto to this day used to describe the Swabians (as the local inhabitants were called).

When I reached nine years of age, my father received good news. A cheque for compensation for the loss of the house in Czechoslovakia arrived. It was for DM 860 which was not a lot but enough to secure a loan from the bank to invest in building a new home. Planning permission was granted on a meadow nearby: the very spot where I used to throw Easter eggs with my friends.

My parents bought two spades to dig the foundations for the new house in their spare time. After a day's work and the evening meal they would pick up their spades and labour until well after sunset when my father would allow himself a treat of a bottle of beer before returning to Gasthaus Rose where he and my mother would continue their tailoring work until the early hours of the morning.

Soon it was 'Richtfest' (the topping out ceremony), when the builders completed the wooden framework of the roof of our house; a little fir tree was decorated with colourful ribbons and placed like a crown on the top of the roof timbers.

All the builders and villagers assembled, and barbecued sausages and beer were handed out to celebrate, helped along by the merry music of an accordion.

Painting by my friend Walter Schimpf

22. CHRISTMAS

The 6th December, St Nikolas Day, was full of excitement in the Rosewirts' pub. We children spent all day pressing our noses against the window, creating puffs of haze – an ideal surface for writing words (and sometimes rude slogans) which we quickly wiped off in case St Nikolas (Santa Claus – a role acted out by a neighbouring friend) found us out. We revised little poems and prayers which we memorised in preparation to recite to St Nikolas when he arrived.

As soon as we heard the heavy footsteps approaching the pub followed by the assertive banging on the door we would vanish, without a sound, hiding under the tables.

Frau Rosewirt would appear from nowhere to pull her children out of their hiding places by their ears. When the time came to recite the verses and songs, our hearts were beating so loudly that it seemed to drown whatever was left of our shaky voices.

What was to be the judgement? Was it going to be the whip from Knecht Ruprecht (helper to Santa Claus) for being naughty children or presents from St Nikolas for the good ones?

We all had a conscience for one reason or another.

Although I was the only child who still believed in Father Christmas, the whip, which was always generously handed out to the older children, made it a frightening and very real experience for everyone.

Christmas Eve was the highlight of the year. During the afternoon Emmi and I were locked out of the family living room to allow the 'Christkind' to decorate the huge Christmas tree, a ceremonial occasion for my father. Anxiously and full of expectations we awaited the ringing of the church bells announcing six o'clock, at which time the door of the living room was opened and we were allowed to enter.

It was always a magical moment to see the Christmas tree as tall as the ceiling, beautifully decorated with silver balls, polished red-cheeked apples and the long Lametta immaculately arranged by my father, reflecting the warm flow from real candles. At the foot of the tree a crib was set up surrounded by presents. My father was always overcome by this moment and his whole body would shake quietly and tears would stream down his face.

It was the only time I can remember seeing him cry; no doubt remembering the many Christmases that he had had without family, living only on bread and water. After singing carols the family would finally be seated at the beautifully decorated table and a Christmas prayer was said, which seemed to be never-ending, and the feast began.

The main course consisted of carp, supplied by a travelling fishmonger. This was then placed in a bathtub awaiting the attention of a neighbour who obligingly hit it over the head and killed it; an act that no one in the family could bring themselves to do. On one occasion my father choked on one of the enormous fish bones. I was overcome with horror. What if he died? There would be no presents!

After the meal there would be more singing and music with my mother playing the piano (a generous gift from an elderly lady whose crippling arthritis stopped her from playing) and I would accompany her with the recorder. Then came the best part of all: the excitement of opening the presents. Later in the evening at about eleven o'clock the family would set off for the Christmas service in Musberg, a distance of three miles, proudly wearing our new coats, mittens or boots.

The gentle flurry of huge snowflakes falling softly around us as we walked was truly magical. On our return we would eat apple strudel topped with generous helpings of real whipped cream and sip tea to which my parents would add two teaspoons of Austrian rum.

Maya Kraus

23. EASTER

I also believed in the Easter bunny until I was seven years old. On Easter Sundays, the younger children would roam around the poultry yard, the hay barn and nearby fields to search for beautifully decorated Easter eggs and one by one they would emerge triumphantly with their treasures. In the afternoons there would be competitions in the nearby meadow to see who could throw cooked eggs the furthest without breaking the shell. The broken eggs were eaten straight away.

I always enjoyed a healthy appetite and sometimes could eat four to five eggs at a time. It was always a curiosity to me to know why it was that the eggs belonging to the Rosewirt's children survived this rough treatment better than any other competitor. I later discovered that their eggs were cooked in onion peel which apparently imbued the eggs with a hardening property. These were happy and exciting times!

To this day, my family still carries on this tradition.

One Easter Sunday, when I was seven years old, my Auntie Hilde arrived from East Germany. In those days only female relations were allowed to leave their country to visit relations.

She came equipped with only a small bag and 'a plan': her mother Mizzel, my father's aunt, had left the same morning as Auntie Hilde, taking her two grandchildren, Hartmut and Wilfred. They took the train to East Berlin. At that time it was still possible to be issued a day pass into West Berlin. It all went well. Once in West Berlin they made their way straight to the airport and this is how they were reunited with all of us. The children, thinking this was a great adventure, were very distressed when they were told, only after their arrival at our house, that they were going to stay in West Germany. They threw tantrums and wanted to go back to their friends. They even refused to go out with me to throw Easter eggs, in case the Stasi was coming to arrest them!

Three weeks later their father, my Uncle Rudi, arrived. He had left the house on the same day as his family with the pretence of going to work. He was unable to tell his neighbours and not even his best friends about their plan. His progress was slow, since he could only walk by night. Finally, after spending over two weeks walking over the mountains, he managed to cross the East German border safely, although he told us about many hair-raising moments when he was almost caught.

Both my aunt and uncle were teachers and managed to find work at a school nearby.

24. MOTHERING SUNDAY

Mothering Sunday was always on the first Sunday in May. Edi and I together with Senta (the butcher's dog and faithful friend) would venture out into the Seven Mill Valley to pick wild flowers. We would then arrange the flowers in a bowl, creating a centre with forget-me-nots with their golden hearts, and surrounding it with primroses. Then we would present our gifts to our respective mothers which were always received with moist eyes.

The Valley of the Seven Mills
by Walter Schimpf

Maya Kraus

25. ONCE A CATHOLIC

The community I was brought up in was all Protestant but my family was Catholic. On Sundays a Catholic priest was invited to hold the mass in the local church at seven o'clock in the morning. Every other Sunday service was held in a nearby village in Musberg. This meant that the family Altrichter had to get up at 5.30 a.m. in order to arrive in time.

Again, the cart was pulled out to accommodate Granny because the steep hill proved too much for her breathing. In the early days there were only six families attending the church and I noticed that all the grannies had either a large goitre or were stooped forward like my own granny. One day I made a great faux pas. I accompanied a little friend to a Protestant mass and was seriously scolded by my parents.

Matters became very serious indeed when my stepsister, Emmi, announced at the age of seventeen and a half that she intended to marry a young man called Fritz who was not only a 'Schwabe' but also a Protestant. The age of consent at that time was twenty-one years.

One day the doctor was called to examine my father's mother.

On leaving I overheard him tell my parents in the corridor that her condition was very serious and that she urgently needed a gall bladder operation.

I popped my head through the door where my granny was sitting and noticed that her 'aura' was very weak and her face had a yellow complexion. What if she died without receiving the priest to attend to the holy sacrament of the last rites? She won't get into heaven and meet the angels! I clearly recalled the visit of the priest the day my Oma Berta died.

I returned to my room and placed a candle, a little pot of oil and a serviette on my mantelpiece and then, without telling anyone, I arranged for the local priest to visit us. His arrival was met with polite surprise which turned to shock, especially so for my grandmother, when he explained the reason for his visit! Sadly, she died one week later whilst being operated on for her gall bladder.

26. MY MOTHER (MUTTI) IN TROUBLE

One day on returning home from school, I found my mother in great discomfort. She was suffering from a severe pain on the left side of her abdomen. Without hesitation and without knowing or understanding the term, I diagnosed appendicitis.

My father dismissed the idea, explaining that the appendix is on the right side of the abdomen but I continued, in an agitated manner, to insist that I was right and that a doctor should be called for immediately, even adding that if nothing was done I would call for the doctor myself. My father gave way and called the local doctor who arrived within ten minutes and immediately ordered an ambulance to take my mother to the hospital. On the operating table the appendix burst, causing infection. Happily my mother was saved just in time but she had to stay in hospital for another four weeks. Everyone was amazed at my knowledge of my mother's problem and none more so than myself.

It was my first encounter with a realisation of some kind of gift, which I now call 'psychic healing energy', and this gift was to be called upon on many occasions in my life, although I didn't make anything more of it.

Shortly after the recovery of my mother from the burst appendix and the septicaemia that followed, she suffered a very serious accident.

One morning, when she was pouring boiling water into a large coffee pot, the base of the pot broke and the scalding water ran over her left leg. She was wearing thick woollen stockings – the only type of stockings available at the time – and the wool absorbed the boiling water, compounding the pain. A doctor was called and he applied cold water compresses and he attended for several days afterwards to change the bandages.

Unfortunately the condition worsened and pus formed on the leg, which the doctor scooped away. I wasn't allowed to look. My mother developed a high temperature and became delirious, seeing fire everywhere. The doctor took my father into the corridor and I overheard him say that in order to save her life she would need to have an amputation.

On hearing this I ran into the forest as fast as I could and sat under my favourite fir tree. I asked God for forgiveness for all the naughty things I had done and sought help for Mutti. I waited and after a short while I heard a voice in my head – Honig (honey). Of course! I was always given honey whenever I suffered from a burning throat.

I ran home and told Granny that Mutti needed honey on her leg.

She was mildly amused but she chose to ignore me and soon after my mother was admitted to the hospital. By good fortune, my father knew a doctor working at the hospital and was able to seek his opinion as to treatment for my mother. The doctor told him that a course of treatment, which had proved beneficial in past cases of severe burns, was the application of compresses soaked in honey!

After five weeks of this treatment my mother's leg was saved and had healed, although it was badly scarred, and she was able to return home.

Maya Kraus

27. A NEW FRIEND: THE VIOLIN

During my mother's convalescence I became quite carried away with a new friend, my violin. Herr Kehrmann, who was the choir-master of the local Gesangverein (choral society) which my parents had joined, came once a week to teach me and I remember feeling very special when he told me that there was no need to hold a book under the bowing arm – a technique he had to endure while studying with a renowned Russian teacher – because I held the position perfectly.

Nevertheless, this new interest meant a restriction on my freedom because every day I had to practise for two hours, often with my mother sitting next to me, whilst being aware of my friends enjoying badminton outside the house.

I particularly enjoyed playing anything with semiquavers and, whenever there was a slow passage, I found great delight in gradually speeding up, much to the annoyance of Herr Kehrmann. "Langsam," (slow down), he would shout, but there was no stopping me. Largo became allegretto, allegretto became presto.

In addition to the violin I was also taught piano by Herr Kehrmann. This meant that I had to miss an extra hour of free time.

This new discipline was short-lived, however, as with every lesson Herr Kehrmann's hand would work his way progressively upwards on my thigh so that I became almost paralysed with anxiety, leading to a serious and fatal loss of concentration. I refused to continue with the piano lessons but carried on with the violin.

This gave me a strategy which I knew could be useful, if needed. I could always poke him with my violin bow!

28. SCHOOL AND WORK

At the age of eleven I passed the entrance exam to the Mörike Gymnasium, the only grammar school for girls situated in Stuttgart. I had to get up at 5.30 in the morning to catch the tram in time for the start of school at 8 a.m. By this time my violin playing had improved considerably and I was invited by the local priest, Pater Sieber, to play at weddings.

Every Saturday morning he would collect me and we would set off on his Vespa to the wedding venue. He had a wooden leg due to a war injury and this gave the ride a certain unnerving unpredictability. Shifts in balance had to be negotiated which was not always easy when clinging on with one hand and carrying a violin in the other and it happened on more than one occasion, especially in the winter, that we ended up sliding into a ditch.

On one occasion, after enduring a long journey in heavy snowfall, my fingers were so frozen that I shivered uncontrollably during the playing of Ave Maria. Afterwards, the mother of the bride came up to me and with tears in her eyes, congratulated me on my beautiful vibrato and gave me an extra 3 DM!

Maya Kraus

29. THE CIRCUS

I used my modest earnings from playing at weddings to learn horse riding, which I had always wanted to do. Unfortunately, 'proper' horse-riding lessons cost DM 5 and, since I only earned DM 3 per wedding, I was forced to compromise and without telling my parents, for fear that they would not approve, I enrolled in a circus riding course which cost exactly DM 3.

This was my second excursion into the magical world of the circus and, although I harboured some misgivings about my deception, I was very excited. The circus riding was taught by an acrobat who had deserted a travelling Hungarian circus. I enjoyed every minute of it. I loved the romance and colour of the circus, the glamour of show business and the muscularity and strength of the horses, especially their smell.

The course taught mainly bareback riding with no shoes which involved handstands, a scissor action and other daring exercises. The only means of contact with the horse were two iron hooks fixed to a roller around the horse's girth line that offered some stability. Using an old mattress for a base we practised handstands and various others exercises.

The circus master was very encouraging to me. He would interlock his fingers of both his hands to create a cradle for me to step on. He then would lift me up onto the horse. Eventually I learned to mount the horse by myself.

As I gained more experience I was introduced to my first circus skill. The horse was made to gallop around the arena and I had to run alongside it. Once I gained the right rhythm and speed of the horse I jumped up as high as I could and just about managed to reach the hooks to pull myself up with.

One day the programme involved the building of a tower involving six participants and, being the lightest and suitably agile, I was chosen to be the pinnacle of the tower. This meant that I had to climb over three friends who formed the foundation, followed by another two at the next level and then take my position at the top where I had to stand tall with my arms stretched out. All went well and the tower was achieved and the horse was led to move forward by the circus master.

Unfortunately, unknown to anyone, the horse had a graze on its leg which attracted some flies and in an attempt to 'shoo' them away the horse jerked, causing the tower to collapse and throwing me about twelve feet to the ground, injuring my neck and back.

It took me five harrowing hours to complete the journey home across meadows and fields that would normally have taken me only two. In those days there were no telephones or transport from the stables and I was reluctant to be discovered for my deceit. This was the end of my circus riding and the start of a painful period of discomfort which kept me in bed for many weeks at a time during the school years to come. It was also an interruption to my violin playing apart from a few starts and stops whenever my neck obliged.

We often gave performances in various little towns and villages and received many acclamations and praise for our performances in the local papers. Fortunately for me, my father only read the 'Stuttgarter Nachrichten' and never found out about my change from riding to circus riding. I know he wouldn't have approved.

Maya Kraus

30. MUSICAL AMBITION

In time the restriction caused by the circus injury improved sufficiently to enable me to continue with my violin lessons. Unfortunately, my original teacher, Herr Kehrmann, had died after a fateful manual colonic irrigation, and my father arranged an interview with a well-known teacher and member of the Stuttgart Philharmonic Orchestra to further my studies. He listened to me with great interest but told my father that in all fairness he could not take me on as his pupil as I was 'way out of his teaching domain' but recommended that a teacher at the Music School in Stuttgart would be a good idea.

Off we went to the academy to meet the director. When I approached the entrance to the Music Academy I froze. The building was as black as black could be and was still bearing scars from the many bombing raids that destroyed three quarters of the town. My father tried to coax me by promising me a new winter coat and a camera but there was nothing to move me. He even threw in the promise of a new pair of roller skates but I was adamant; there was no way I was going into that brooding dark hole!

Maya Kraus

31. A GOOD LESSON

Injuries and absences from school apart, which made me often to lie still in bed for two weeks at a time in pain, I managed to glide through all the growing pains of a teenager.

I was, by nature, an optimistic person believing in a glass half full rather than half empty and this served me well. I had managed to catch up much of the work in most of my studies with the exception of physics, which presented me with great problems. I had harboured the idea of studying medicine but, despite extra tuition, I had to accept in the end that it wasn't to be. By this time I had had enough of study anyway and was restless to get out into the 'real' world.

I declared that it was my intention to leave school and get a job. To my surprise my parents offered no resistance and were very supportive. My father even arranged for me to work at Speik, a well-known soap factory during my summer holiday. The work consisted of smoothing the rough edges of soap which were exposed when combining two halves of soap together.

All day long I sat in front of a conveyor belt peeling the overlapping remnants of soap away with a small knife.

It was like peeling potatoes and the conversation among the other workers around me was stifling, confined mainly to gossip about the antics of film stars and, of course, the opposite sex. I lasted no more than two weeks and gave my notice in. The supervisor was very disappointed, claiming that he thought I had picked the work up very quickly and showed great promise. I decided to resume my studies. Little did I know at that time that my father had conspired with a friend of the company to 'set me up' knowing full well that I would get bored of the work very quickly.

When I was eighteen years of age I was ready to take the big step of becoming independent. I wanted to travel and experience other parts of the world and having considered my options I decided that I would go to Switzerland to study languages at the University of Geneva.

32. MAYA THE RACING DRIVER

A chance meeting with an old school friend whilst shopping in Stuttgart introduced me to the exciting world of motor racing. My friend's name was Bernd and over coffee where we recounted old times and exchanged news he told me of his ambition to become a racing driver. He was extremely passionate about it and his enthusiasm was so catching that when he invited me to 'enjoy a spin' at a local racetrack I accepted eagerly and agreed to meet later that week. Bernd warned me not to eat too large a breakfast!

The racetrack had the curious name of 'Solitude' which was a complete misnomer, given the assault on the ears from the noise of engines. It was a fully competitive racecourse where serious events were staged but on non event days it was given over to members of the public who wanted to experience track conditions or simply to practise driving techniques.

Bernd's car was a Volkswagen Beetle but with modifications so that the engine was tuned like a racing car. The roar from its engine was deafening and as we set off around the track the power of the car surged through my body. And all the time Bernd was giving a running commentary on performance and technique. It was wildly exhilarating and at that moment I caught the racing bug!

Having recently passed my driving test I asked my father if I could borrow his car without giving any indication of my purpose. It was the same model as Bernd's but without modifications and happily my father agreed. With a sense of excitement I set off to the racing track and booked myself in. My first few circuits were tentative, to say the least, but as my confidence grew and the 'hints' I had gained from Bernd came into play, I acquitted myself very commendably, even though I say so myself.

On returning home my father came out of the house to greet me and immediately expressed alarm. "What have you done to my car ?" he asked. "The tyres are hot and there is a smell of burning rubber." I searched for a plausible answer and explained that I had to make an emergency brake. My father looked at me steadily but made no challenge. From then on, however, I was only allowed to drive his car with him as a passenger.

Even to this day and whenever possible I like to watch Formula 1 motor racing on TV. I love to relive the sense of excitement I had experienced and – I just can't get enough of it!

33. MY FIRST LOVE

There was, however, one event in my life that I still hold dear. It is the experience of first love. It happened when I was sixteen years of age and I met the man of my dreams. Sadly it is not a story with a happy ending but rather, a story of what might have been.

It was carnival time and the local village hall was the venue for a masked ball. Since I had nobody to take me I couldn't attend but I decided I would go to see what was going on. I stood on the steps of the entrance of the foyer and admired the colourful spectacle of the people inside, rather like a fan at a film premiere watching the stars. It was an exciting time but I also felt very isolated and after a while I decided it was time to leave for home. It was then that I saw him: the man of my teenage dreams.

He was so handsome with lovely eyes and beautiful bone structure and, like me, he was not in carnival dress. He wore a white collarless shirt and a black waistcoat and looked princely. Our eyes met and held briefly and then he was lost among the dancing crowd. I felt almost dizzy with emotion and disappointment but then I became aware of him making his way towards me. He smiled warmly, asked me to dance with him and led me into the main hall. It was a magical moment, straight out of a romantic novel you might say, but it was happening to me.

I learned that his name was Hansjerg and I also learned that he was born a Swabian and a Protestant. I was suddenly overcome with fear remembering my sister's dilemma and parents' heartbreak when she declared her intention to marry a man in the same circumstances. I asked him whether he was an artist and played the piano. This surprised him and he wanted to know how it was that I knew of his interest in art and of his enjoyment at playing the piano. I replied that he had 'piano hands' and that I could see him in my 'mind's eye' working on a canvas.

Our friendship continued and we met a few times at my home to play duets. One day he announced that he had been asked to perform a Chopin waltz to celebrate the birthday of a distinguished professor and he asked me to take part and to play some of the duets we had worked on. It was a wonderful occasion and our performance went very well.

Afterwards we waited for his sister to collect us but she did not turn up, so we decided to make our own way home along the railway track, jumping from one railway sleeper to the next. He offered to carry my violin and when he put his arm around my neck in a comforting way I felt paralysed. I so wanted to respond but I froze. My experience of young men was very limited and I didn't know how to express my feelings for him much as I wanted to.

When we approached my house my father was pacing up and down outside and was very agitated because of the lateness of the hour. He made his displeasure very clear to Hansjerg and forbade him from contacting me again.

I was devastated. Every morning after, I woke up with a heavy heart. I found it difficult to concentrate on my schoolwork and I spent hours dreaming of Hansjerg and sketching his face in order to feel close to him. My life had suddenly expanded and I didn't know how to fill in the gaps. I didn't wash my neck for several weeks to treasure the traces where he had touched me but, in time, my mother noticed it and in a determined manner neutralised the memory with a hot wet face towel.

A few weeks later I saw him briefly during my final school's dinner and ball at the Liederhalle in Stuttgart, to which parents were invited. It was customary for the final-year students of the boys' school to join with the girls' school (one year younger) to take up dancing lessons. It was literally 'boys meet girls' and both sexes were very shy with each other. We girls planned and designed our own ball gowns for weeks ahead and my parents paid for me to visit a professional hairdresser for the occasion.

On the night I felt quite pleased with myself that the most handsome of the boys had asked me to be his partner.

Everyone was seated waiting for the main course when I spotted Hansjerg. He waved to me and gestured to follow him upstairs. I excused myself on the pretext of needing to visit the toilet and joined him on the first floor and away from prying eyes where we danced to the music of Johann Strauss played by the house orchestra.

I was thrilled and yet full of guilt at the same time. I wanted him to know how much I had missed him but I thought of my parents, their hardships and how my sister's marriage had upset them deeply. I didn't want to hurt them, even though by then my sister was now happily married and had presented them with two granddaughters who were adored by my parents. They had also come, in time, to accept their son-in-law.

We could only allow for one dance since my parents and my dance partner were waiting downstairs. Some months later we met again. One day out of the blue, Hansjerg visited my family home and presented me with a big parcel.

"This is a painting I made for you," he said.

I was so overcome with emotion that I became tongue-tied and all I could produce was a timid "Thank you". At that point my mother appeared and, after a polite exchange of greetings, my prince left forever

34. THE BONE MAN – MY SAVIOUR

One day, my father drove me to a remote little village nearby where he had arranged an appointment for me to see a 'bone man' who had gained a reputation for helping people with spinal injuries and associated pains. The venue was an old farmhouse and my father had been instructed to arrive after dark, which struck a curious note, and to bring a bedspread to be used during the examination.

When we arrived at the farmhouse we were met by the farmer's wife who explained that the 'bone man' had helped her to regain full movement in her legs and that she no longer required a wheelchair. In gratitude she had arranged for him to occupy a room in a converted barn to continue his work.

We were led to the barn and directed to climb up a ladder which provided access to a small, dimly lit room where we were greeted by a tall, middle-aged man with a gentle manner and kind eyes. The bedspread was positioned over a long wooden table and I was asked to remove my clothes down to my underpants and to lie on my front.

He stroked his hands very gently over my spine and after a while I heard him say to my father that my problem was not in the neck but that he could feel a displacement of the vertebrae in my lower back.

He ran his hands up and down my spine and then followed this by massaging my whole back very firmly. All of a sudden I heard a loud click followed by a second click in the lower region of my spine. When the treatment was finished my father sought his advice with regard to a planned family holiday to the mountainous area of southern Tirol in Italy. The 'bone man' confirmed that it would be perfectly okay for me to travel and that the altitude and the sunshine would help provide extra vitamin D which is so beneficial to the promotion of good bone structure.

We set off two days later for the holiday and, on reaching the long winding road up the Brenner Pass, my whole back and neck were hurting so much that I begged my parents to stop the car to allow me to rest and lie down at the roadside. When we finally arrived at our holiday destination I felt so sick with pain that I forewent dinner and went straight to bed where I prayed and cried myself to sleep.

The following morning I was woken up by the sun shining on my face. I carefully moved my head and, since I did not experience any pain, I slowly sat up. Still no pain. I made my way to the window to look outside. The sky was a pale blue with specks of lone clouds drifting beneath like cotton balls.

Gentle sweeping hills led up to a big mountain range, all lit up and robed in its early morning light of orange and yellow. Deep down in the valley below there was a sea of apple trees climbing up the valley, their pink and white blossoms bursting with bloom, filling the air with a sweet scent and beckoning me to come out to explore. Slowly I walked downstairs, still in my nightdress, and I found the front door unlocked and stepped outside.

I gradually allowed my body to move to and fro – still no pain. Then I followed a little path down towards the valley along a grassy slope dotted with little white star-like flowers. I can still remember to this day the sensation of the refreshing morning dew under my bare feet, as I was bouncing off the mossy grass - still no pain.

The steep slope invited me to go faster until I had no option but to run in order to keep my balance and not to fall over. I ran and ran with my arms spread out, feeling the gentle, soft and soothing alpine wind passing through my outspread fingers, my nightdress swaying behind me, tears streaming down my face. I felt alive – I was flying! Afterwards, it was a long way back up the mountain, just in time to change and to join my family for lunch.

Three weeks later and still without any discomfort, my father and I returned to the farm for a follow-up appointment with the 'bone man'.

We were met by the farmer's wife who told us that the 'bone man' was no longer present. She explained that a woman he had treated had experienced greater pain after her treatment (as I had done) and as a consequence had complained to the police about his activities. The 'bone man' was subsequently arrested for being a bogus medical practitioner and sentenced to a term in jail.

35. GENEVA

Geneva, elegant, sophisticated and cosmopolitan with beautiful buildings, restaurants, shops, cafés and of course the beautiful lake, was another world to me and so much bigger in all respects to the relatively sheltered life I had left behind.

I had settled into my university course, made many new friends and had found a room at the Maison des Etudiantes which I shared with a group of girls all under the watchful eye of Madame. I had also remembered to bring my friend the violin with me and was able to play it in my room when I knew it would not disturb others.

I was eighteen years of age, fully independent and I had the feeling that the world was my oyster! It was a glorious time, but I was to learn that oysters can live in troubled waters.

Maya Kraus

36. A STRANGE ENCOUNTER

One day, on my way back from university, it was raining heavily and I kept my head down to avoid huge puddles when all of a sudden my umbrella bounced off another one. I stopped, as did the other owner, and when I looked up I found myself face to face with a very good-looking young man who apologised and greeted me very politely.

From his accent I knew he was French. I noticed that he was carrying some piano music under his arm. I was so charmed by his manner I hesitated to move on and pointed to his music and mentioned that I was a violinist. He told me that he had just returned from the 'Radio Genève' where he performed one of Chopin's Nocturnes.

We spent some time chatting in the rain and he suggested that we meet up again at the pavilion in a nearby park at five o'clock the next day. I was so excited and could hardly sleep that night. Could he be the Adonis of my life?

Of course I was far too early for our rendezvous and I walked around the park. I didn't want to arrive at the pavilion too early and give the impression of being keen. At exactly five o'clock, I walked up the steps to the pavilion. He was not there. I waited for over half an hour and there was still no sign of him.

I was on the point of leaving when he suddenly appeared, advancing towards me in a great hurry. I was so pleased to see him and smiled warmly. He bounded up to me and struck me very hard on my left cheek and as he turned away he shouted: "Now you know how my mother felt under the Nazi occupation!"

I was stunned and stood completely paralysed for a long time. I could feel my cheek burning and the side of my face swelling. It was very painful to touch and I couldn't stop crying. When I relayed this incident to my parents some time later they explained about the persecution of the Jews by the Nazis and the horrors of the concentration camps, which until then I had not fully comprehended.

37. UNDERCOVER POLICE WORK (TRAITE DES BLANCHES)

This is a story I have never shared with anybody. I have kept it a complete secret until now. I was having morning coffee with a girlfriend in a café when we were approached by two men who started chatting us up. They were amusing and silly and it was all very playful but I wasn't entirely comfortable with the situation.

After a while, I indicated to my friend that perhaps we should be on our way but she was reluctant. I stayed a little longer and, at an appropriate moment, once again suggested to her tactfully that we should leave. She clearly thought I was being a spoilsport and she suggested quite pointedly that I leave, adding that she would follow when she was ready.

I was not happy about it. Something troubled me about the situation but I left anyway.

After a few days when I had not heard from her, I checked at her lodgings and was told that she had not been back since we last met. This did not make sense to me as there was no reason that I could think of why she should not have used her lodgings or indeed left no indication of what she was up to.

With some apprehension, I phoned her parents hoping for a positive response but they had not seen her nor heard from her. My apprehension turned to serious anxiety and when I enquired at the university and learned that she had not attended her lectures, I knew that something was seriously wrong. I turned to the police and their reaction can only be described as startling. I was whisked into a private room, and in the presence of three or four plain-clothed men, I was questioned in depth on what I knew.

They were very serious and professional but I could sense their excitement. They pressed me for every detail: place, time, description of the men involved. When they had completed the interrogation they informed me that lots of girls had gone missing and they were aware of an underworld gang abducting them and most likely trafficking them abroad.

Then the fun began. I say fun because that is the truth of how I felt at the time. The police asked me if I would be prepared to work with them and to act as bait to trap the men involved. They assured me that I would be under surveillance at all times and that my personal safety would not be compromised. My heart raced with excitement. I was to be an undercover agent in a real life drama. This was the real thing such as I had only seen imitated on television or film and read about in thriller books.

I cannot remember giving any thought to the plight of my friend which, on reflection now, is almost too distressing to think about. I readily agreed to play my part.

The setting was a replay of the original situation. I sat alone with a coffee reading a college course book. There were several other customers in the café. I knew one was my surveillance officer but I couldn't work out which of the customers it was, except I had the sneaky feeling it was the one pretending to read a newspaper!

For a while nothing happened and I was beginning to think it wasn't going to work. Quite suddenly, however, two men, both in their mid-twenties, sat at my table and started to tease me about the book I was reading. I recognised them but fortunately they didn't recognise me or, if they did, it didn't seem to worry them. They talked at length in a personable manner, always attended by good humour and displayed a very plausible interest in me.

I remember thinking that the transition from chat-up line, from first introduction to something bordering on friendly intimacy, was very skilfully crafted and seamless. They spun a story that was innocently seductive about one of their mothers being in a nursing home. They said she would only get taken out for a ride in the car with the promise of lunch at a celebrated lakeside restaurant at Lausanne on the French side of Lake Geneva.

I was told to meet at an address which was duly given to me and was told to bring my passport. It was all smiles and warmth and I remember each of them giving me a kiss on both cheeks in the French manner as I left.

I had been instructed by the police to always make a detour on my way home to my lodgings ("at all costs do not return straight away to the police station"). Later I passed on all the information I had gained to the police.

When the morning arrived for the rendezvous I sought out the address I had been given. It was in a quiet, respectable area with attractive, cared-for houses and displays of geraniums in window boxes. It was hard to equate the gentility and air of respectability with the menace I knew it harboured. There was little sign of activity around; the occasional walker, a strolling cat, but I did notice a car parked just a little way beyond the house that I was making for. A young couple were embracing with some relish. They appeared to only have eyes for each other although I knew better.

I walked up the short flight of stairs to the front door and rang the bell. The door was opened by a woman, roughly in her early forties, who was clearly expecting me. I was invited in and she closed the door behind me.

My first impression was shock. The interior was quite run down, not particularly clean and the furnishings were cheap as though the house had been fitted out from a bargain warehouse. I was led up a flight of stairs to a landing and then let into a room where I confronted the two men from the café. The room smelled of cigarette smoke and stale beer and the curtains were partially closed so that it all seemed rather dim. The two men greeted me with cool detachment. Gone was the charm and easy humour. They wanted to know if I had brought my passport with me as they had instructed me to do. When I replied that I had not, they became extremely agitated. One of the men grabbed my arm in a rough fashion and sat me on a chair and gagged me. The pair of them started arguing in a coarse manner in a language I didn't understand.

One of the men picked up some photographs from the table and displayed them to me. At first I didn't understand what the pictures were about. The images did not make sense to me and then I realised they were close-up photos of an extremely pornographic nature. I turned my head away in disgust.

Suddenly we all became aware of a commotion outside the room followed by loud knocks and a rattling of the door handle. It was the first time I realised that the door had been locked.

Then there was the most almighty crash, the door flew open and in rushed several men whom I realised were non-uniformed policemen. The scene was chaotic but unfortunately (yes, I mean unfortunately) I didn't have the chance to see exactly what happened because I was led out of the room and out of the house by a policewoman. Outside the house there were policemen in uniform, one of them with a dog, and there was a conspicuous black police van with its back doors open.

Looking back now the whole business was clearly extremely dangerous, particularly given that it might have gone terribly wrong but I was young and had a propensity for being impulsive (some might say reckless) and my naivety was my shield.

I thought little about it afterwards and continued with my studies at the university and enjoyed the pleasures that Geneva had to offer. One day, however, I received an unexpected reminder that brought the whole episode into sharp focus. A letter arrived at my address by a courier expressing thanks for my cooperation and enclosed was a generous amount of Swiss Francs, towards the expense of a new coat (mine was red).

It was a very welcome bounty as I was obliged to do part-time work to support my studies and pay for my lodgings.

Most importantly it provided enough to pay for an airfare to England in order to study English.

This would allow me to fulfil another ambition of mine: to become an air hostess. I was delighted by my good fortune but I remember being advised by a police officer that it might be wise, as a precaution, to dye my hair a darker colour and to find alternative digs.

Maya Kraus

38. ENGLAND, HERE I COME

In January 1964 I found an au pair placement in London where I had to look after a delightful two-year old boy called Gabor. His father was Hungarian who worked as an engineer and his mother was a nurse.

Although I was welcomed warmly into their family, I couldn't stand my freezing bedroom. There was no heater in my room and very often I went to bed wearing my white fur coat, socks and a hat.

The other problem was that on my day off, if I wanted to travel to the West End to go to the cinema, I had to leave before the end of the film in order to catch the last tube train back to Archway. I managed to stick with it for three months. When I was offered a job for four months at an international translating agency in Oxford Street, I gave notice and left the family. I still feel bad about it.

I found new digs sharing with three girls in Kensington, West London. It was and still is a very upmarket part of the capital and not only did it allow me to stay and watch the end of the films but it placed me within easy reach of some of the most prestigious shops in London, including the famous store Harrods in neighbouring Knightsbridge.

I also learned new etiquettes. The English don't use condensed milk in tea or coffee and when making tea the milk is poured into the cup first, whereas the opposite is true when making coffee. I also discovered, to my delight, that dunking biscuits in tea or coffee was acceptable and with practise I managed to perfect this art, always removing the biscuit before it collapsed.

On the question of manners the English shake hands only when first introduced unlike the Germans, whereas in France a handshake could be accompanied by a series of kisses on both cheeks!

I also found that the English are very polite when it comes to mispronunciation or using the wrong word which as a foreigner coming to terms with a new language happened to me quite often. On one notable occasion when addressing my hosts I thanked them for a lovely evening, for an excellent meal and for being so hostile!

New courses in the proficiency of English only started in September and in the meantime I was looking around for another part-time job. One day I passed by the Olympia Exhibition Hall and noticed that it was advertising a food fair for two weeks. When the bus slowed down a little, I jumped off and heard the bus conductor shouting after me.

I entered the huge exhibition hall and enquired of the steward whether there were any vacancies but was told that all the positions had been filled. I pleaded with him to check to see if there were any cancellations.

The young man looked through his book and, noticing my accent, asked me where I was from. "You are lucky. There is still one vacancy with a German lady who doesn't speak English and needs someone to interpret for her." The lady told me that she had escaped from East Berlin where she was a theatre director. In order to make a living she had created some waterproof paint in various colours, which could be used on shop windows for advertising. She was handsome rather than attractive and I was fascinated by the fact that she always wanted to brush my hair.

As we got to know each other better she often invited me to visit her at her flat although, I never did but for no other reason than I was extremely busy. It was only much later that I came to appreciate that her interest in me was more personal than professional. I had never encountered lesbianism before and was more intrigued by the revelation than shocked. It made little difference to my attitude towards her. I respected her for the kindness and integrity that she showed towards me.

Maya Kraus

39. MEETING FRANK

Next to us at the food fair was a young man who advertised small red packets of crisps called 'Walter's Potato Puffs'. He introduced himself as Frank and handed me a small tub of delicious ice cream that he had secured from a stall opposite to us, which was run by two beautiful Icelandic girls.

This was a welcoming refreshment since the hall on the first floor was baking with heat and was absolutely airless. I thanked him and thought to myself that he was quite nice-looking but not enough to make my heart skip a beat, besides which I felt sure that his main interest was the girls on the ice cream stand. When our eyes met, something touched me deep inside. His eyes had a somewhat familiar twinkle. They were blue/grey with tiny golden specks which looked like little jewels. Later during my studies in iridology, I learned that these markings were indeed referred to as jewels.

At the same time, I sensed a sadness buried deep inside. I remembered seeing this quality of sadness before – in my father's eyes. I looked at the surrounds of his body and found that there was a dark distortion in his lung area and I knew that he had vulnerability in this area.

Very often from early childhood I experienced seeing this 'grey film' around certain people and if it was distorted I knew it indicated something worrying but I never mentioned it.

One day Frank told me that he would not be manning his stall the next day because he had to enrol at the Holborn College of Law for his solicitors finals. I was genuinely surprised. This man who was selling potato puffs from a stall and keeping me supplied with ice cream was super-intelligent! My interest in him took on a new respect. As we talked I mentioned that I was looking for a course to improve my English and he said that he knew just the place and asked me for my details.

When we next met he once again presented me with an ice cream and told me that he had enrolled me in a course of English for foreign students. I was thrilled and asked him where the course was to be held. He smiled warmly and with a mischievous twinkle in his eyes told me it was the Holborn College of Law. We were to study at the same college. How very convenient! Of course, we met up every day for lunch at the university canteen and it wasn't long before we started dating.

One day I was in the college refectory as usual for lunch but there was no sign of Frank. This was unusual and disappointing as it was my birthday.

I began to have doubts. Could it be that he was cooling off? Perhaps seeing too much of each other had not been a good thing. I was preparing myself for the worst when all of a sudden there he was, his eyes sparkling and grinning like an excited schoolboy. He handed me a Marks and Spencer bag and wished me a happy birthday. Inside the bag was a lady's jumper which he had been prompted to buy because there had been an occasion earlier when I had been feeling cold and he had lent me his. I asked him how he knew that it was my birthday. He laughed and told me that he had made a special note of it when I had given him my personal details needed for my enrolment onto the English course. My pleasure must have been obvious to him although he knew nothing of my earlier misgivings.

That same evening we went to a pub in the King's Road, Chelsea, for a modest celebration. It was a very lively scene, full of happy people enjoying themselves. We sat near a group of musicians and I became fascinated by the lead singer who was playing an instrument that I had never seen or heard before. It was a couple of spoons! To my surprise Frank went to the bar and collected two spoons and accompanied the singer. I had no idea he was so talented! He even sang in tune. I particularly remember a rendition of a well-known Cockney song 'Daisy, Daisy, give me your answer do' which seemed to be delivered with such personal directness that I felt my cheeks blush.

At the end of the evening Frank walked me home. It was only a relatively short distance and we held each other closely. We were wonderfully happy and our mood matched perfectly with the romance of late-night London with its easy seductive charm. Arriving at the door of my flat I hesitated for a moment. My encounters with men from early childhood had conditioned me to be cautious. I knew Frank was keen but he had never placed any physical demands upon me of an intimate nature and I was never made to feel uncomfortable.

He was always the gentleman. I had no doubt that what he felt for me was genuine and for my part I felt safe with him. He was caring, warm, extremely funny and confident which appealed to me. I really didn't want the night to end. I was 'romantically ripe' and ready (and curious) to experience the 'great sexual adventure' that occupied the intimate conversations of so many of my girlfriends. It was the time for 'Daisy' to make up her mind and I did. After all, it was my birthday!

40. INTERVIEW FOR AIR HOSTESS

Having applied to become an air hostess with Pan Am, I received an invitation to attend an interview at the company's main office in central London. It was such a glamorous job and I was very excited and allowed my imagination free reign. I savoured the pleasures to come, the worldwide travel, meeting lots of different people of different cultures and the very real possibility of meeting Yehudi Menuhin. I was in seventh heaven and very naïve.

I took great trouble to make sure my appearance was appropriate; neither overdressed nor underdressed and selected a very smart navy blue outfit that had been designed and tailored by my father. When it came to the interview I found that my interviewer was a woman. I had no reason to believe that the interview would not be conducted on very professional lines but somehow I felt that the absence of 'sparkle' between the sexes was an inhibiting component. It was a very formal procedure and when it concluded I was thanked for attending and that was that. It was hard to judge how things had gone but I did not feel encouraged.

Maya Kraus

41. A GREAT SURPRISE

When I returned home to Germany for Christmas to be with my parents I found a letter waiting for me with an American stamp. This had to be a response from Pan Am following my interview. I was so excited and a little apprehensive.

Would it be good news or a rejection? I opened the envelope carefully and retrieved the folded letter. I felt a charge of joy overtake me. I had been accepted to work as an air stewardess starting in March. This was my long-held ambition, my dream, and it had come true. I wasted no time in sending my letter of acceptance.

It was more surprising then that from such high spirits I found myself shortly afterwards feeling extremely tired and I often stayed in bed until lunchtime. My appetite, which had always been very healthy, now deserted me. My parents were very concerned and arranged for me to see the local doctor who after examination declared that I was perfectly fit but that I should be encouraged to eat heartily as I was now eating for two!

My parents took the news well, rather better than me in fact, because I had no choice but to write to Pam Am and withdraw my acceptance and there was the very serious consideration of whether to tell Frank.

I had no idea how he would respond to the situation particularly as he was still studying for his lawyer's degree and had no income. My parents made it clear to me that they would offer whatever support I needed including, if I chose, arranging an abortion in a clinic in Switzerland. It was an absolute no for me although to my shame I remembered a friend from Geneva who found herself in a similar predicament bringing about a termination by lifting a heavy sewing machine and I tried the same strategy using my father's very heavy irons used for pressing material. Thank God it didn't work. I told the little baby inside me: "You are here to stay and I will love you always."

After Christmas, Frank invited me to join him in Paris where he was staying with friends to celebrate the New Year. I accepted the invitation partly because the prospect of seeing Paris was agreeable and I was anxious to be with Frank and explore my feelings for him and, perhaps equally important, his feelings for me. I took the train to Paris and was met by Frank who greeted me warmly and with enthusiasm. He was eager for me to meet his friends and to show me around the city which he loved.

When we reached the Eiffel Tower, I declined to walk up the many steps as I was so out of breath. Frank was surprised as I had always exuded great energy and he asked me what the matter was.

I told him that in Stuttgart the altitude was different and I needed a little time to adjust (a little white lie) and encouraged him to go up by himself while I waited at the lower level. I was feeling very sick but I didn't want to spoil things for him and I certainly didn't want him to know the real reason for my deception.

That night we celebrated with his friends and at midnight we saw the new year in with champagne. Frank told me that he was very sad at the prospect of my leaving to go to America; that he was worried I might meet a wealthy cattle rancher and forget all about him. He then became quite serious, which was unusual for him, and I didn't know what to expect. He told me that he wanted to marry me as soon as he finished his studies and would I be prepared to wait? It was a proposal. I told him that waiting was out of the question and that if he was sincere he would have to hurry up as he was about to become a father.

It was quite a situation for both of us. There was a moment of hesitation as he took in this news and assembled its implications and then his face lit up with pleasure. He put his arms around me and held me in a warm embrace. And that was that. The new year had arrived and we were engaged! I phoned my parents to tell them the news and they suggested a family celebration. I knew they were happy for me but I also knew that they were keen to take a look at this young Englishman who had won my heart.

Introducing Frank to my parents proved to be a great success. I had felt some apprehension that they might hold him to account for the situation we found ourselves in or that he was not of the same faith, but my worries were unfounded. They liked him and were very happy for us. There was a moment in this first meeting that endeared him to the family when he thanked my mother for a delicious lunch adding that he thought the food was "schrecklich". It was a case of unintentional comedy. He had often heard his parents, who spoke German with their friends, say, "this was terribly nice" a compliment. Terrible in German is translated as 'schrecklich' but Frank had omitted to add the word 'schön' which means nice.

At the invitation of my parents, Frank's father travelled to Stuttgart. I arranged to meet him at the train station and, although I had neither met him before, nor had I seen a photograph, I recognised him straight away. He was much taller than Frank and a sturdier frame. He was well dressed and he had the bearing of a worldly man. I introduced myself which surprised him. I think he was expecting to be met by my father. He asked me how I knew it was him. I said that I recognised him by his eyes, which was true.

42. FRANK'S FAMILY

Frank's grandparents owned flourmills and a biscuit factory producing 'Kraus Biscuits' and 'Bretzels', which were well known all over Czechoslovakia. Being Jewish they were aware of the danger they and their family were in from the Nazi persecution and as a precaution they arranged for their sons Walter and Willy to travel to England. For themselves they considered that their position in the business world, with its influential social connections, would spare them any attention from the Nazis but it proved to be unfounded and they were transported first to Theresienstadt and finally to Treblinka in Poland where they perished.

Frank's father Walter and his brother Willy settled in London. Despite holding a doctorate in law, Walter was not allowed to practise English law and so he had to consider other means of supporting himself. What better than to call upon his family background as successful bakers? He set about making biscuits in his home kitchen and he sold them in Shepherd's Bush market and local shops and they became very popular.

Encouraged by his success, he approached the Western Biscuit Company and impressed the directors with the quality and originality of his biscuits and as a consequence they offered him a contract.

He was now on his feet financially but his greatest triumph came when he invented an original product which became famous, known as 'Walter's Potato Puffs'.

Its success, which owed much to the sponsorship of the Western Biscuit Company, led to the establishment of a factory in Shepherd's Bush. During this time, he met and fell in love with a girl called Melanie who, like himself, had been born in Sudetenland and had grown up on the other side of the mountain, just a few hours' walk away from where I was born. She too had come to England as a refugee. Her brother tried to escape to the East and sadly was killed in Hungary by the Russians.

Walter and Melanie married and had three children, Robert, their firstborn, followed by Frank and then a daughter, Esther. Sadly, Robert died in a traffic accident on the M1 motorway. The car in which he was a passenger crashed into a lorry which was stationary and displayed no lights. His parents never got over the grief.

43. THE WEDDING

Our wedding took place on the 2nd February 1965 at Hendon Registry Office. Frank and I had been living in a room in Frank's parents' apartment and it was from there that we were to be picked up in a car provided by one of Frank's friends. My parents were unable to attend as my mother was unwell with pneumonia and my father felt that he should stay with her. Frank's mother was also unwell but thankfully Frank's father, sister and an aunt did make it to the wedding.

Frank looked extremely handsome in his new suit. By choice he was happiest in casual clothes but I think he surprised himself by the distinction the formal dress gave him and, on more than one occasion, I caught him posturing in front of the mirror, although his gestures were invariably comic. I wore a soft cream dress with a matching jacket with blue forget-me-not motifs. I had chosen to wear my hair raised into a bun secured with a small adornment of freesias, which matched my bouquet of freesias. Frank remarked that we would look dandy as a decoration on a wedding cake!

When the car arrived I could hardly believe my eyes. It was a gleaming Buick on loan from the wealthy father of one of Frank's friends, Vere, who now became our chauffeur, complete with official peaked cap.

It was all very luxurious and great fun and we felt like famous film stars on our way to a premiere, which in fact it was.

On the way to the registry office I experienced a moment of doubt which I found unnerving and unwelcome. The car stopped at some traffic lights in Shepherd's Bush displaying red and, whether it was real or imagined, they remained red for a long time. I could feel myself becoming more and more anxious as the time passed.

Why wouldn't it change? Is it an omen? Is it something telling me to reconsider, warning me even? I stared desperately at the red light, which remained impassive. How long could this go on for?

I could feel the tension building up inside me and I remember checking the road to see if it would be safe to open the door to make an escape. Then suddenly the lights changed to green and the car moved on. It was as though I had been tested and, having passed, was allowed to move on.

Frank sensed my unease and squeezed my hand reassuringly. He looked at me with his sympathetic eyes and said, jokingly: "You had your chance there." I returned his smile weakly. It was just a moment of 'weak knees' and no more.

The wedding was truly fabulous, thanks in large part to many of Frank's friends who were such a merry crowd and were determined that we should have a great time. We had the reception at a restaurant called the Black Sheep and there were both formal speeches and lots of impromptu speeches of a humorous and teasing nature. It was such a happy occasion and even the February weather was kind to us.

When the party was over I fully expected to return to Frank's family home but there was another surprise in store for us, as our 'chauffeur' drove us to a garage. I believed that this was in order to fill up with petrol, but it was not so. Waiting for us at the garage was a small car with the words 'Just Married' written on the back window. I was given the keys to the car (as it was known that I held a driving licence) and told that in the glove compartment we would find an envelope with some instructions.

When Frank opened the envelope it contained a copy of an insurance certificate and the address of a hotel where a room had been booked for the night in our name. It was so wonderful and a complete surprise to both of us. Everything had been taken care of by Frank's friends including a huge bouquet of gladioli which greeted us when we checked into our honeymoon room.

The following morning, after a leisurely and not so early breakfast, we prepared to return the car to the garage. I drove the car out of the driveway of the hotel and turned right on to the main road. We hadn't travelled very far before Frank enquired in a very casual manner whether I had managed to pass my driving test first time. I was very proud and told him that I had indeed passed first time and asked him why he had asked. He replied by pointing out that I was driving on the wrong side of the road!

44. FINDING A HOME

I had spent many weeks searching for somewhere to rent and concentrated my search on the district of Holland Park which I thought was a particularly pleasant part of London. Unfortunately I had no luck. As soon as it became clear to the various landlords that I was pregnant the door was shut in my face, sometimes quite literally, and I noticed several houses that posted notices in their windows stating 'no children and no blacks!' I eventually found a two-bedroom flat in Hornsey, North London. It offered very basic amenities but it meant we could leave Frank's parents' apartment and become independent.

Life was a struggle, as the little money we had spare from my earnings was swallowed up by an electrical heater. In those days landlords were allowed to adjust the meter and charge extra. The cold autumn and winter months that followed caused Frank to suffer severely from asthma (a problem I had detected on our first meeting) and he was on numerous antibiotics and inhalers. Our bedroom had no heating and the bedroom walls were so damp I had to wipe the mould off each morning. When my parents visited us they were so shocked at the conditions they saw that they gave us a cheque to cover the down payment to enable us to buy an apartment. This was a great sacrifice on their part because it represented their life savings.

We moved to Acton (Frank jokingly referred to it as the 'industrial wasteland of West London') and set up our own home. This came just in time. House prices moved up to 70% and very soon after, the average house became up to 10 times the previous value. 'Borrow now, pay later' was an invitation from mortgage lenders for an easy access to obtain a mortgage.

Thereafter followed a series of energy crisis: the Arabians created a power shift and there was a 70% price rise in oil. It became a free for all. An all-out miner strike plunged everyone into darkness and inflation went up to double figures.

45. THE BIRTH OF PAMELA

I managed to find a job at Futurum in Baker Street as a secretary. My knowledge of shorthand in 3 languages came in useful. I also attended a course of the newly established National Childbirth Trust once a week in the evening to prepare myself for the arrival of our first child. When the time came it proved to be a very difficult delivery for both of us. After thirty-two hours the midwife called a consultant who noticed that the baby was facing down the birth canal with her neck bent backwards. After a successful operation he saved our lives but I was left with countless stitches, even in the back passage, and found it very painful to move about. It took me ages to climb down from the tall hospital bed to settle the baby who cried often and there was little sympathy from the other mothers in the ward who cast irritated looks in my direction.

In those days there was a strict rule in the hospital that feeding should take place every four hours. This seemed to work for the other babies on the ward but my baby became distressed after two hours with the result that the nurses simply wheeled her away from me. I could hear her crying in the corridor every time someone opened the door to the ward. Eventually we were both allowed home. We were now a family and we had a beautiful daughter whom we named Pamela. But the crying continued whenever she woke up, which was almost every hour.

I walked her about trying to comfort her and I was crying myself with worry and exhaustion. I thought maybe I was not a natural mother and yet I loved her so much.

In those days there was no support for young mothers. I gave up breastfeeding and introduced bottle-feeding but the situation did not improve. In desperation I went to see my GP who assured me that I had a normal healthy baby and that things would improve in time. The crying didn't stop and I noticed that whenever I came near her I felt a sharp pain around my navel. At first I put it down to anxiety but I became convinced that it represented something significant and went to see my GP again.

This time I saw a different doctor and I asked him to check Pamela's tummy. "Can't you see the black spikes coming out of her navel?" I asked. The GP looked at me oddly, no doubt thinking I was crazy, but he did make an examination. He confirmed that there did seem to be a problem and made some phone calls to arrange admission to a hospital as an emergency. She was operated on the same afternoon. I was told that she had an umbilical hernia and if left untreated, it could have been life-threatening. She now has the most beautiful belly button in the world!

46. ENTERPRISE

Money was still very short and I found a job typing envelopes which paid the grand sum of five shillings and sixpence (approximately 26 pence in today's money) for every hundred envelopes. I bought a manual typewriter for three pounds from a junk shop in Acton and set to work. This enabled me to organise my time around caring for Pamela. After three months of relentless typing, I developed severe inflammation in my wrists, recognised today as repetitive strain injury, and was referred to hospital for treatment. I returned with one arm in plaster and the other heavily bandaged. This was the end of my typing career and the income it had provided.

Eventually, after one year of many sleepless nights and living only on coffee and chocolate bars, I suffered from a nervous breakdown. I couldn't sleep, I lacked energy and I had great difficulty breathing. I was also close to tears all the time. I visited the doctor to get some help. He showed hardly any interest. There was little eye contact and even while I was explaining how I felt and without even taking my blood pressure, or checking my general health, he was writing a prescription for Librium (a tranquilliser) which I continued to take for eleven years. I became so dependent on those nasty little oval green and black tablets that I even carried some spares in a little locket around my neck.

Sometimes and as if out of nowhere, I would break out in a terrific and very frightening panic. My heart rate would accelerate and from time to time miss a beat only to restart with an alarming bump. My legs turned to jelly and breathing became a desperate and frightening struggle.

Interestingly, whenever I was pregnant, I managed to stop taking Librium, but as soon as my children were born I got hooked back onto it.

It was the era of the Swinging Sixties and youth culture, a boom time for the permissive society, when Britain was emerging from the drabness of the post-war era. The designer Mary Quant contributed fun in fashion by creating the revolutionary and liberating miniskirt (named after her favourite car – the Mini) and hot pants. She had judged the mood of the country astutely, recognising the desire for colour and excitement, particularly among the young, and she tapped into the growing confidence of the national economy which meant more money for clothes and luxuries.

Then along came BIBA. When Barbara Hulanicki and her husband, Stephen Fitz-Simon, moved from their first shop in Abingdon Road, Kennington, to Kensington Church Street, their shop became so popular that one had to queue outside and wait for someone to come out in order to squeeze inside.

Sadly in 1971 the Angry Brigade placed a bomb inside the store. Then BIBA moved to what was formally known as Derry & Toms in Kensington High Street. This was a most attractive building and BIBA's products were well suited to its art deco design. Here you could find clothes, wallpapers and paints displayed over seven floors with each area having its own theme. I found it particularly amusing to visit the mothers-to-be department where tall hat stands and oversized chairs, tables and ornaments were displayed in order to make pregnant women feel more in proportion and therefore more comfortable. An imaginative case of downsizing!

There was also the children's department displaying a doghouse with a giant Snoopy. Most exciting was the area where one could try out make-up for free. This was a great innovation and I wasn't the only one who would avail herself of this opportunity before going out to work or a party without feeling embarrassed. On the fifth floor you could dine at the Rainbow Restaurant or hang out on the Roof Terrace where, if you were lucky, you would glimpse the presence of pop stars.

It was an extraordinary time of creative dynamism and I wanted to be part of it. But what could I do? There was certainly a need to do something because with no income from typing envelopes and Frank still working towards his finals, our savings were dwindling fast.

Maya Kraus

47. KINDLIN' CANDLES

I had an inspiration. It was two months before Christmas and the only candles available in the shops at that time were either fat or thin, in red or white.

I sent Frank to the Price's candle factory to research how much stearin in ratio to candle wax was needed to create a non-dripping candle. At the same time I contacted Marimekko in Finland, whose colourful and fabulously designed clothes I had admired from magazines, and asked if they would be prepared to give me the name of the company who supplied the dyes for their clothes. The company was very generous and provided the information I sought and I wasted no time in placing an order for dyes, which arrived within a week.

I set to work, heating the candle wax in a large pot over an open gas fire and employed empty baby food tins as moulds which I filled with various different stripes of colours of candle wax. This was a very Heath Robinson operation in such a confined kitchen area and looking back it was not without its dangers, especially as I was pregnant with my second child and my belly protruded in prodigious circumference. It was an extremely industrious period and I was filled with excitement borne of a sense of entrepreneurial spirit.

During this time, I negotiated with the manager of the indoor Kensington Market to rent a space. The negotiation took the form of a generous bribe which was an early lesson in the creative dealings of commerce but it was worth it. The indoor Kensington Market was an extraordinary building which housed many small stalls over two floors. Young designers and artists were selling anything from hand-knitted pullovers and cardigans, home-made pottery and batiks, colourful Indian dresses and even second-hand fur coats purchased from old ladies who presumably had no further need of them. It was here that I saw the first sale of blue jeans which before had been regarded as workmen's clothes. I even managed to persuade Frank to wear a pair of purple flared jeans with tiny stars imprinted on them.

The problem was where to find the money for the deposit to rent the space in the market. It just so happened that we were approached the next day by a film producer who showed interest in buying our little Citroen, a 2CV, for a Saturday matinee film (very popular at that time) and waved £50 pounds at us, just the amount needed for the deposit and one month's rent in advance.

We didn't hesitate, since the offside door, wing mirrors and the number plates were held together with Scotch tape and there was a big hole on the floor of the passenger side as when we had offered a huge lady a lift, she went straight through it. The film producer also mentioned that should the car, which was to be haunted by a ghost and driven by a stuntman, survive a run down a hill we could have it back. Needless to say, we didn't hear from him again. Pity, because the registration number was TOY 28 and worth more than the car.

Now we were up and running and Frank decided that we needed a name. He had noticed a newly established shop selling doughnuts on Shepherd's Bush roundabout called Dunkin' Donuts. He suggested we named our business Kindlin' Candles, which I thought was very witty.

I phoned many embassies to acquire the names of candle manufacturers abroad and then followed this up by phoning the various companies and asking for samples and price lists. I claimed that I had just opened the first dedicated candle shop in London. To my surprise and delight, I received an array of attractively carved and decorated candles. Some came from Austria with beautifully carved rose motives and from Eika Candle Company in Germany I received a dozen carved candles in various sizes. From Scandinavia, I was sent candles that glowed from within and from Mexico I received an enormous shipment containing black totem poles, twelve inches tall with silver motives painted over enormous wings. I sold all the samples and placed orders for more.

The expression 'selling like hot cakes' was very appropriate.

I was approached by the son of the owner of Jacey's Cinemas, who liked my candles and had just opened up 'Jacey Galleries' at Marble Arch. He invited me to display my candles in his gallery. It was a wonderful opportunity and I was very excited at the prospect but I had to decline because I couldn't afford the rent for such a prestigious setting. I thought that would be that, but to my amazement he asked me to join the gallery for no rent. It was an offer I couldn't refuse. Everything was moving very fast and I was extremely busy but I still relied upon Librium to enable me to cope.

Like the proverbial buses that come in threes, this invitation to display my wares in Jacey's Galleries was followed by another from a distinguished gallery in Bond Street, which I also accepted. Business was booming. I now exhibited in three venues and had taken on staff to keep them running. I had also negotiated a very significant order with Woolworths, subject to a finalisation of price. I appeared in Women's Own magazine wearing hot pants and knee-high boots, standing next to a one-metre tall candle, in a natural brown colour, displaying a beautifully carved Bacchus, the god of wines, which I had imported from Germany.

We purchased a second-hand minivan to help me to get about and I painted the roof with psychedelic flowers – after all, it was the era of the hippies, 'flower power' and women's lib (the liberation from wearing bras).

People started using 'grass' and, if they could afford it, LSD. A number of enthusiasts from the UK left for Drop City in Southern Colorado, a utopian place, where they could live their dream world'. Soon after, Drop City became a popular outing for spectators who came in busloads wanting to witness naked people (although this was not so, as I was told by one of the hippies) and, after ten years, the inhabitants had to abandon their abode.

For me in London, things were almost too good to be true. And so it proved to be. There were more lessons to be learned about the world of business, the principal one being the relationship between supply and demand. The sale of candles had worked extremely well leading up to Christmas but afterwards the demand dropped dramatically.

It all came to a grinding halt though. We were dealt a fatal blow when the government, in its wisdom, raised the level of purchase tax. Even more significantly, for a business that relied on foreign supplies, it also raised the import tax, resulting in an overall price increase of fifty per cent.

The result was that we were priced out of the market and could no longer supply imported candles for Woolworths, John Lewis and other shops. The business was no longer viable in the long term and within a few months we were once again relying on savings to survive.

The arrival of our second child, a boy whom we named Simon, the absence of any income from Frank who had yet to qualify and the need to find money to pay the mortgage took its toll and my reliance on Librium continued.

Kindlin' Candles was snuffed out.

Kindlin Candles
3 Emanuel Court
Westbourne Avenue
London W3
01·992·2926

48. IF AT FIRST YOU DON'T SUCCEED

It was a chance meeting with an Australian visitor to London that saved the day. He approached me in Kensington Market and asked if I would be interested in selling earrings that he had designed. It was a strange encounter given that I was dealing in decorative candles and there were other traders in the market dealing in jewellery. Perhaps he judged that business was slack and I would have the time to listen to him or perhaps he sensed that I would be sympathetic to his overture.

Whatever the impulse, it proved to be very successful for both of us. His designs were very simple silver-coloured earrings of various sizes. Above all they had two winning features; they were attractive and cheap. I agreed a commission on sales and designed a display board covered in black velvet, which showed off the earrings. They were an instant hit with trendy young girls who snapped them up enthusiastically. Often I would arrive in the morning to open my stall to find a waiting queue of eager customers.

Inevitably the time came when the traveller, having tolerated the English climate with good humour and fortitude, decided to return home. We had established a good business relationship which had served us both well but obviously whilst the demand was strong the supply posed a serious problem.

Trusting in our friendship, I asked him if he would mind sharing with me the technique for making the earrings. His response was more than generous and very surprising: "Just wrap a wire around the top of a chair, cut it, shape it into a ring or a loop and insert the fittings."

Armed with this knowledge I went to Hatton Garden and purchased a reel of wire, some cutters and various pliers and fittings. However, the tops of our chairs at home were square and I had to think of a solution. I used a rolling pin for the large earrings and the handle of an apple corer for the smaller sizes. It worked a treat and I set to work using a trestle table as a workshop in the bedroom. Then I became more ambitious and introduced a 'ring within a ring' and 'loops within loops'. Later still, I added colourful beads and this inspired my product name of **Marikka Handmade Jewellery** as a tribute to Marimekko. This was the name of the Finnish fashion house whose colourful designs had so impressed me when I worked in Helsinki as a secretary for three months with the Lutheran World Federation's World Assembly, during my university holidays. There was no limit, other than the imagination, to the variation of styles that could be made up.

When I was approached by a buyer of Peter Robinson, Top Shop and BIBA, who ordered a gross pair of every design, I had to revise my working system. My apple corer and rolling pin had to be abandoned.

My wrists had still not recovered fully enough to cope with the extra manipulative demands the bending, shaping and cutting would involve. After some research I identified a factory in Sheffield capable of designing a machine that could cope with shaping the various sizes I needed. It enabled the productivity to increase to such a degree that I was able to employ local housewives on a part-time basis and set up a cottage industry.

Encouraged by the success of the jewellery business I wanted to extend my knowledge and skill and I enrolled in evening classes at the Isleworth Polytechnic to learn to become a silversmith. One evening at the college, I was summoned to see the head of the jewellery department. Apparently, since I was the last person seen who had used the centrifugal casting machine, I may have placed the powerful blowtorch wrongly into its holding place. Instead, the flame was directed towards the kiln. The flame gradually had worked its way into the thick wooden base, built in order to support the heavy kiln. Luckily, the night watchman noticed a suspicious smell and, after investigating, called the fire brigade. They managed to extinguish the smouldering wood, which could have caused the kiln to plunge down through the first floor ceiling...

Whilst studying at the college, I also obtained a goldsmith licence from the company of Johnson Matthey in Hatton Garden which allowed me to purchase gold at eight pounds an ounce and I incorporated this into my designs. I did receive a very pleasing accolade when I learned that a ring designed by me had been accepted for an exhibition at Goldsmith Hall and had been admired by Princess Margaret. It was never made clear to me whether she had actually offered to buy it but in any case it was intended for my mother and had an offer been forthcoming, I hope I would have made the right decision.

Through an introduction of a friend I met the Hungarian artist Dr. Arthur Fleischmann. He had not been allowed to study art and, instead had to finish his studies in medicine. Once qualified, he put away his medical books, came to England and concentrated on sculpture. At that time when we met, he worked on colourful pieces of Perspex which he assembled in abstract designs to create huge water fountains which he exhibited at St James's Park, London.

He was looking for a silversmith who could use his material and create silver surrounds for smaller pieces to be worn as necklaces. We instantly became friends for life. I met very interesting people who wanted these pendants and I also made a brooch for the wife of the Australian ambassador.

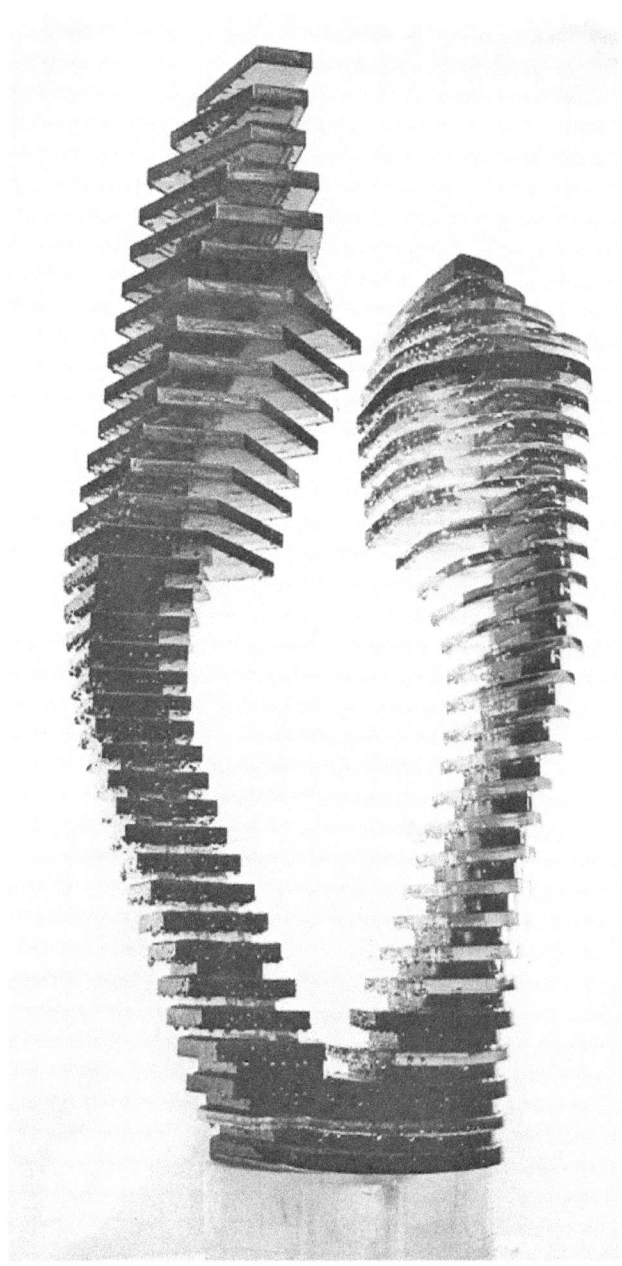

One of the water fountains

Maya Kraus

49. CHOKERS AND CHAINS

I had the idea of making a plain silver band which could be worn around the neck to match my silver earrings. I worked out a simple way of fastening it and then put it to the test to see if it could be worn safely whilst asleep.

I asked Frank to listen out in case I started choking but happily, come the morning, the ring was perfectly okay and so was I.

I enhanced the design by adding hand-dyed beads and more intricate silver designs and I called them 'CHOKERS'. They are still called the same to this day! They had immediate appeal and I had a job to keep up with demand.

One day I arrived at Kensington Market and noticed a street trader standing by the entrance with a tray displaying my very own earrings and chokers with the declaration 'Made in Hong Kong'. I was livid! How dare anyone steal my designs and then have the effrontery to sell them within the vicinity of my own shop?

But there was nothing I could do. I didn't have any copyright on my designs and I couldn't afford to challenge the issue in court and anyway it was pointed out that it only required the smallest variation in pattern or even a simple scratch mark to avoid violation of my work.

It was Frank, with his sound sense of proportion, who calmed me down and offered me good counsel. "If you can't beat them then stay one step ahead of them." I took his advice and explored the idea of making small delicate silver- and gold-coloured metal chains, simple designs at first and then more elaborate layers of chains which I cut into various lengths and in which I incorporated silver and golden beads in various sizes. They looked beautiful and soon everyone wanted to wear them – including men! I had started the chain fashion which spread all over England.

A friend of ours was Roger Cook, a musician and songwriter who became famous overnight when he wrote the popular Coca Cola song: 'I'd like to teach the world to sing'.

Roger asked me to make a dozen chains of various lengths with beads for him to wear at a forthcoming concert. "Keep the beads fairly loose, so that I can tear the chains off my chest and throw the beads to the audience."

I never witnessed this scene but I was told it worked a treat. All the youngsters screamed whilst trying to catch them from their idol.

As I knew full well, it did not take long before the idea was copied and could be seen on sale in markets and shops all over town. I was resigned to it but I did gain some satisfaction in knowing that my designs were original and that I had made a contribution to the swinging London scene.

With all the new contacts we made our circle of friends extended. One day a young American, Carole Stansill, opened up a stall opposite me. She sold her own designs of hand-made batiks that I admired. We were both pregnant at the time, me with Oliver and Carole with twins. We instantly fused and started a great friendship.

Since the time when, as a small child, I diagnosed my mother's appendicitis, I had experienced countless premonitions of accidents and disasters. I didn't welcome these experiences and tried to pass them off dismissively. One afternoon when I was invited to Carole's home she showed me a recent delivery of two baby cots, a baby buggy for two and various baby clothes. It was a hot summer's day but suddenly I felt very cold all over and had a sense of foreboding. Naturally I didn't express any concerns and helped her move everything into the newly decorated nursery.

One week later she lost both her unborn children due to serious complications. It was part of a double tragedy for Carole. Her husband was the editor of a magazine called 'IT'. At the same time, by unhappy fate, he was being prosecuted for allowing homosexuals to advertise. To avoid a possible prison sentence, they went abroad overnight.

I heard this from Carole many months later, by virtue of a postcard from Ibiza in which she delighted in the 'simple life' and asked me to write to her soon. Sadly, she omitted to include her address. I still treasure the large batik she gave me as a present entitled 'mother and child' and which is now displayed prominently in my home today.

Journey of a Healer

Maya Kraus

50. MISS FRENCH

There were, of course, many other events happening during this time. The most notable was the birth of our second son, Simon, who arrived two years after Pamela.

Next came the birth of Oliver who 'popped out all in a rush' two years after Simon. Both boys were delivered without complications at the Queen Charlotte Hospital in Hammersmith – known locally as the 'baby factory'.

We were now a family of five with all the attendant concerns and responsibilities. For me, despite the demands of the jewellery business, the family always came first. I made it my responsibility to take them to school and to collect them and to show an interest in them as individuals. I knew from my own childhood how important it was to be loved and I took inspiration from my parents. It was not easy and I had to organise my days to get everything done, which often meant getting up very early in the morning and working late at night. And I was still 'popping' Librium. It was all dancing and jiggling. I didn't want to micro-manage my children and I had to use quiet discipline!

Once the jewellery business had got established and there was an income, I was able to employ a nanny to help. She was an Irish girl, rather proper in her sensibilities and 'fair bait' for my spirited children who took delight in shocking her by bending over and exposing their bottoms. After this nanny, we employed a French au pair called Françoise. She was both very attractive and very capable and she delighted the children by teaching them some simple French phrases. One day she asked me if it would be okay to fill her spare time by giving private French lessons. Of course that was perfectly okay with me and I suggested that she put an advert on the local school's noticeboard.

Very soon afterwards I kept getting all these peculiar telephone calls from strangers asking for 'Miss French'. I became very irritated and used to slam down the phone whenever it became clear that it was another nuisance call. On one occasion I decided to find out what was going on and when the call came with the same enquiry I asked the person where he had got my telephone number from. He replied (the callers were always men) that he had got the number from a toilet at a North London Tube station and that the advert read 'French lessons in your home by Françoise'.

I twigged at last what these calls were all about and told the man that it was my private number and he should hang up, to which he replied that it would be okay with him, he was quite prepared to pay for a threesome! After questioning Françoise, she admitted to having ignored my suggestion and placed an ad in a local newspaper shop instead. When I went there, it read: French lessons with Françoise in your home, followed by our telephone number.

And then there was a woman in her sixties whom I engaged to do some housecleaning. She was a regular Mrs Mop. She wore a headscarf with protruding curlers and was a chain smoker (only too apparent when I discovered burn marks on some of my fabrics) but she set to work with vigour. I learned much later that she had something of a reputation for entertaining 'gentlemen friends' and one could only wonder at the vitality of her hospitality! It did, however, explain (or suggest) why it was that the bathroom felt rather clammy on her working days and why my perfume – some of it very expensive – seemed to be evaporating at an alarming rate.

At last Frank finally qualified. It had been a hard slog but it meant that now there would be another income which was very welcome and enabled us eventually to move to another, larger house in Acton. Frank had hoped to find employment with a private company but the best offer came from Hammersmith Borough Council and he accepted. The best offer he got from a private firm was eight pounds per week whereas Hammersmith Borough Council offered twelve pounds per week. (At that time our weekly housekeeping bill for basics was £5 per week.) Frank stayed with them for a number of years, completing his articles before being successful in securing the position of assistant town clerk to Surrey County Council in Guildford. This brought about yet another house move out of London and into the country. It was not a change that I felt entirely confident about, despite the fact that I had spent most of my time as a child living in deep countryside. I was concerned that the locals would not accept a German girl in their community but as it turned out I was simply revealing my insecurity – no doubt based on previous experiences which had gone deep – and I was welcomed with great kindness.

After a period of renting, we found a house we liked in a charming village nestling in the Surrey Hills with a pond and ducks and surrounded by beautiful open countryside. The house was a small cottage with delightful period features and in the garden we discovered a large wooden summer house which we divided into a workshop for my jewellery and a playroom for the children. At a later date we extended the cottage and added a conservatory to house my exotic plants and so it became a spacious family home. Soon after there were two new additions to the family – two gorgeous and mischievous dogs, Sandy and Rory.

From here I would commute each day to London to continue my jewellery business but the demands of being a mother, wife and businesswoman were taking their toll and I was still dependent on the pills to keep me going.

Something had to give and the catalyst came from an unexpected and distressing piece of news. A good friend of mine from Stuttgart had committed suicide. Her name was Dolores and I had known her since I was a teenager when we played together in the semi-professional Stuttgarter Liederkranz Orchestra, whenever my sore neck allowed.

Her childhood in Switzerland had been very unhappy. She had an obsessive mother who forced her to practise the piano relentlessly until she herself became an obsessive perfectionist. Whenever the mother went out she would tie Dolores to a chair to prevent her from escaping. But escape she did by eloping with her music teacher at the age of seventeen and moving to Stuttgart where our friendship began. Whenever I returned home to see my parents we would meet up and spend time together. On one of these occasions she confided in me that she was not happy in her marriage.

Later I was to learn that she had taken her own life by driving her car into the forest where she attached a hosepipe to the exhaust of the car. She was found clutching a photograph of her nine-year-old daughter. The news shook me badly and from that moment I closed down my workshop and stored away my tools, never to pick them up again. I was deeply upset and, as I had done before when in need of solace, I turned to my faithful friend – the violin.

This was the second time I had encountered the tragic death of a friend. When I was sixteen years old, my parents and I travelled to Vienna to visit the only living relation of my father, Monsignor Josef Altrichter, a priest who devoted his life to the poor. He was one of nine children and had learned to survive with only the bare minimum. He had transformed the ruins of a factory and set up a home for sick and crippled children. He slept on the floor using cardboard packaging as a mattress and covered himself with thin remnants of blankets. On leaving, my father gave him a new coat.

My parents and I stayed at a bed and breakfast accommodation where we were served by a girl, who was just one year older than me. We were immediately attracted to each other and enjoyed each other's company.
I had noticed that my new friend, whose name was Renate, was often seen with red, swollen eyes as if she had been crying. I admired her for her beautiful wavy long hair and her amazing large, sky-blue eyes and long black eyelashes. When I asked her to join us for a boat trip on the lake, she said that unfortunately she had to work.

After our return home I suffered from very stressful nightmares. They were always the same: I found myself in a dimly lit cellar with Renate crouched in a corner and a tall man standing next to her. She would then turn her head towards me, her eyes begging me to help her. When these nightmares continued I asked my parents to spend the next holiday in Vienna again and afterwards relaxing by the lake at the same B&B where Renate lived. My parents happily obliged.

Once in Vienna, we visited my father's uncle again and found him half-asleep on his 'make-shift bed. Nothing had changed in his room since the last time we came. When my father asked him, why he didn't use his coat for cover, he told him, in a frail voice, that he gave it to a poor man, who needed it more than him. I could tell from my father's facial expression that he was 'quietly' very upset.

Renate and I were overjoyed to meet again. She had lost a lot of weight and I felt that I had to find out why she was so sad. When I asked her father to allow Renate to come out with me for a walk by the lake, he replied that she had to do bookkeeping.

It was only after I persuaded my Papa to speak to her father that it was agreed that she could join me but only for one hour after lunch. During the boat trip, when we were sitting by ourselves, I questioned her about this and she confided in me, with tears streaming down her face, that life with her father was unbearable.

"If I make the smallest mistake in bookkeeping or anything else he locks me up in the cellar and abuses me sexually. If I scream, he hurts me. I am so desperate to run away. Please take me with you to Germany. I can clean and work very hard".

I was extremely shocked and relayed the story to my father, who found it difficult to believe at first but came to realise that the situation was serious. Under the pretext of wishing to apply for a passport my father visited the local town hall where he learned that it is obligatory for the father of children to be the signatory, the age of consent being twenty-one. Before leaving to return home my father engineered an opportunity to explain the situation to Renate and to promise that he would arrange for her to come and join us in Germany when she was free to leave.

After two weeks we received a letter from Renate's mother, enclosing an unopened letter that I had sent to Renate and informing us that her daughter had died. When my father phoned her to learn more, she was extremely cautious and insisted that no further approaches should be made. She did, however, explain that Renate had persuaded a friend to take her for a ride on his motorbike and, whilst travelling at speed, some kind of 'incident' had occurred causing her to be thrown from the bike to her death.

51. THE IMPORTANCE OF MUSIC

Music has always played an important part in my life. I inherited a natural feel for music and was encouraged by my parents to develop my ability. I chose the violin because it was easy to carry but even as a child I responded to its ability to express depth of feelings in the most profound way, especially when I heard Zacharias playing Hungarian gipsy music. I showed great promise from an early age and at different stages in my life I was presented with opportunities to play in orchestras and operatic societies of high quality.

During my stay in Geneva I was introduced to Monsieur Henri Dunand, a well-known conductor from Radio Genève, by a friend who had heard me practising my violin in my room. He was very kind and asked me to play something for him. I was very nervous to start with but I became very relaxed once the music took over.

Afterwards, he smiled at me warmly and asked me to join the Jeunesses Musicales de Suisse and to take part in an international music festival being held on the Spanish island of Mallorca. This was very flattering and thrilling and, of course, I accepted. The prospect of seeing another country and getting a taste of its culture was irresistible even if it was a short visit.

It was in Mallorca that I witnessed my first – and definitely my last – bullfight. I could see nothing noble or in the least bit entertaining in subjecting such a majestic animal to barbarous torture. A much happier memory of this visit was winning first place in the festival, which delighted us all. To be considered the best of all the international orchestras taking part was truly a great triumph. After the concert I happened to sit next to Monsieur Dunand on the coach returning to the hotel. He offered me a place in the Conservatoire de Musique de Genève. This was a wonderful opportunity and a great privilege but I knew I couldn't accept because of my neck injury which still caused me great discomfort. Not wishing to seem ungrateful I thanked him and told him that I could not afford it as I had to support myself. To my amazement, he offered to arrange a scholarship for me. This placed me in a difficult situation. I certainly didn't want to offend the great maestro but, as it happened, England beckoned and the situation was resolved.

Once I gave up the jewellery business I had more time for myself and was able to devote more attention to my music, both as a teacher and as a performer. Having settled into our Surrey home, making many friends and contacts, I was invited to join the Surrey University Orchestra which, under the direction of Vernon Handley, enjoyed a very good reputation. It was so inspiring to work with so many young and talented musicians and it was great fun.

During this time I applied to the London School of Music to study for a diploma in performance but I urgently needed a teacher to improve my level of playing. I was recommended to Frederic Buxton, a viola player of the London Philharmonic Orchestra. After a few lessons he sadly died from a heart attack on his way home from playing at Glyndebourne!

Another opportunity presented itself when I took part in the Summer School of Music at Charterhouse School, Surrey. There I met Penelope Morrish-Howard, a tall gracious lady and leader of the Arriaga String Quartet. I asked her if she could give me violin lessons. She told me that she taught at the London School of Music but did not take on private pupils. The next day, when she was coaching our string quartet, she offered to give me private lessons, provided I used a shoulder rest. I always liked to hold the violin close to my body and, reluctantly, although privileged, I promised to buy a shoulder rest. I travelled once a week to Tonbridge to prepare for my diploma.

Eventually I managed to receive my performance diploma, signed by W.S. Lloyd Webber, the director of the London School of Music, father of Julian and Andrew Lloyd-Webber. I felt somehow that in succeeding at this level I had made up for lost opportunities and done justice to the ability I had been given, to my parents and to the many teachers who had helped me from childhood onwards.

During this time Frank and I became more acquainted with the Arriaga String Quartet, which we sponsored to play at St. Smith's Square where they performed for the last time. Harold Strub, who played the cello with the Arriaga String Quartet became a good friend of ours and invited us a few times to his house where we met his two sons whom he cared for. (His wife, whom I had also met previously, had left Harold for a man who could play the trumpet without the instrument, solely by using his voice and lips!)

We knew that Harold was also the leader of the cello section of the Royal Opera Company and that, after performances, he would drive a taxi so he could pay for his boys' tennis lessons. Very sadly he died from a heart attack.

Although all our three children showed great talent in music, the sad death of Harold made me suddenly realize that parental control could get in the way of our children's true calling. I did not want them to end up playing as rank and file players, struggling to make a living. If it was meant to be that one of our children were to take up music as a career, then it was up to them and the universe. So I decided from then on to loosen the reins of their daily practice, very much to the children's delight; at the same time I continued to encourage them to do well and to enjoy music.

As it happened, Simon gained a music exhibition for his trumpet playing and Oliver won a top music scholarship, both from Cranleigh School in Surrey.

Simon went on to London University to study business and finance. He then pursued his career in banking, which he enjoys.

Oliver studied music at Kingston University. Very soon after qualifying he became a sought-after composer and player with various well-known bands. His compositions have also been performed on film and TV and he is now a popular string arranger and performer with various well-known bands.

As for our daughter Pamela, it was quite a different story: By the time she was eleven years old, she had passed grade V in violin and ballet with distinction. She also showed a natural talent in gymnastics and joined the Guildford Sports Centre, as it was known then. Coaches found in her a promising candidate to be trained for the south-east regional championships and she was offered extra free tuition. Sadly, one day, after hard training of two non-stop hours, she fell off the asymmetric bars and broke both her elbows. When I arrived to collect her, I discovered that the only protection below the bars was a thin mat, as used for judo practice. During the court case that followed, we learned that her coach was not even qualified!

This accident left her slightly disabled in her left arm. The movement of her left wrist and elbow rotation was restricted. However, since this hindrance gave her extra movement towards rotating her wrist to the lateral side, we realized that this could be an advantage for holding the violin. Since she was very keen to continue her violin playing, I found a good teacher for her. After passing her A-levels and grade VIII violin with distinction she was offered a place at the Royal College of Music. Shortly afterwards, she fell in love with Gilles, a French concert pianist and gave up her studies at the college and got married to him in France.

My greatest and most rewarding joy has been – and still is – the pleasure of making and playing music with my children, all of whom have inherited a love of music and become accomplished instrumentalists. Frank lists his credit as playing the tape recorder! Family gatherings have invariably found us assembled as a family quartet (with Frank also handy playing the spoons!) plus one, which is as beautiful and fulfilling as family togetherness can be.

52. YOUTH ORCHESTRAS

When my children were ready to join various local orchestras, I found myself on their committees. My son Simon played the trumpet with the Godalming Youth Orchestra where I coached the string section. Sometimes, when the conductor, Peter Clack, was unable to attend (he was a member of the London Symphony Orchestra), I would pick up the baton and conduct the orchestra.

In the meantime my son Oliver was invited to join the Reigate String Orchestra by his cello teacher, Miss Lovell. Oliver had only just joined the orchestra when she approached me to ask whether I could help her to organise a one-week concert tour to Eschweiler in Germany, their twin town, since she did not know the German language. Miss Lovell travelled every Wednesday from Reigate to our house to give Oliver private tuition – how could I refuse?

In Eschweiler we were greeted with a concert performed entirely with accordions. I have only ever come across a single accordion being played to accompany folksingers but over 40 young players on the stage together was quite a memorable and heart-warming experience.

Eschweiler was known for its coal mining industry. We were taken to visit one of these enormous landscapes and learned that brown coal was plentiful and precious for energy production, so much so that they even moved roads and houses to extract coal! It was there that the remains of a dead man from ancient times were found and he was named Neanderthal.

After our last concert I addressed the audience to thank them for our warm welcome and presented the director of music with a glass goblet with our logo (which I had engraved myself with a diamond pen) and finished by saying: "See you next time in England". On my return, I had barely set foot in my house, when the phone rang. It was the director of music from Eschweiler. "We are coming with our accordion orchestra!" Help! What had I let myself in for?!

First I tried to get in touch with Reigate Town Hall to arrange for some concerts and accommodation with families. They showed no interest. Eventually, and only after I continually made a nuisance of myself, they offered accommodation at a little boarding school which was closed during the holidays, but no concerts. I then pleaded with Guildford Borough Council. I informed them that this accordion orchestra had won first prize in a German competition and that the 40 young players were only between nine and thirteen years old. Again I was turned away. What to do? I was so embarrassed. Eventually I found a listening ear with Surrey County Radio who offered us a transmission for an outdoor concert in the High Street,

Guildford, which I accepted with great relief (although weather permitting!) This was definitely not enough to return the warm hospitality we received in Eschweiler.

Then I had a sudden inspiration. Why not approach the BBC's producer of Blue Peter? They were very forthcoming and so it happened that I managed to find a highlight for the visit of the little accordionists. On the screen they looked so sweet like little beetles with tiny heads only just about managing to peep over the huge bellies of their instruments and their busy little fingers making somersaults over their shiny mother-of-pearl keyboards. Some of the children were too small to reach the floor from their chairs and you could see their little legs dangling below, swaying with the rhythm of the music. It was a great success and I was so very proud of their musical talents. They all received tea and cake and were each rewarded with a Blue Peter pen, much sought after by all the little Blue Peter fans in England who wanted to possess such a treasure!

Word got around and I found myself faced with a much bigger project. Soon after, my daughter Pamela and my son Oliver had joined the Surrey County Youth Orchestra, an orchestra which prided itself for its high standard, consisting of over 80 talented young musicians within the county of Surrey (under 19 years of age). During a parent committee meeting it was decided to take the orchestra to France. However, again, there was a language problem.

Suddenly all eyes were fixed on me. France in August, when all the people were away on their long holidays! I set forth with planning an interesting tour, from Paris to the Savoy Mountains.

Frank was very helpful in finding contact numbers of various town clerks and music directors. I put on my posh Parisian accent and managed to secure nine venues. I thought that a highlight could be to play at the chateau where they produce the famous champagne Moët Chandon, and where I knew that they often gave concerts accompanied by fireworks. I found the number of the office of the owner, Monsieur le Comte.

His secretary put me straight through to the great man. He said that he was 'désolé' and explained that they are closed in August. To put on a concert it needed the pompiers (firemen) and various security officers who were on holiday at that time. However, he suggested that I get in touch with his cousin in Paris, who was a patron of Les Amis du Jardin Shakespeare in the Bois de Boulogne, Paris, and that he would arrange to provide some refreshments for the musicians and champagne for the adults. He then gave me the telephone number of the duchesse. I felt very touched and asked him in my best French: "Monsieur le Comte, could I have your precise title so that I can address you properly when I write to you with my thanks."

He replied: "My name is Monsieur le Comte Remy Martin de Chandon Moët."

We had a great time and the young musicians excelled themselves throughout. Although there was not much of an acoustic in the Jardin de Shakespeare, they did themselves proud and played the Adagio for Strings by Barber, Walk to the Paradise Garden by Delius and Bizet's Carmen Suite with great professionalism. And we adults enjoyed a glass (or two) of Moët Chandon champagne, kept in silver buckets filled with ice.

Since all of the French people I contacted accepted our invitation, I ended up with eleven concerts in thirteen days! It was a great success. Wherever we went we were cordially received and spoilt with amazing gourmet dinners: fois gras, petits fours, home-baked meat and fish pies and home-made gateaux, beautifully displayed on long tables as far as the eye could see.

My daughter's future father-in-law, Monsieur Roger Dalmont, a member of the local Rotary Club with connections to staging plays and concerts, was unable to offer us a concert because everybody was 'en vacances'. However, he kindly offered us a stopover en route to visit the wine cellars belonging to his chateau where we were to have lunch. Again it was a culinary experience with even the local butcher offering his famous rillettes and a huge chunk of paté de campagne. Roger was just about to propose a welcoming toast, when I whispered in his ear: "Could you also include a toast for one of the accompanying mothers who has a birthday today?" He asked for the year of her date of birth. "Attendez un moment," he told me and then he rushed into the huge mouth of his enormous cellar. Finally he emerged with a number of red wine bottles from the year 1938, still covered in cobwebs!

When it was time for me to respond to thank everyone for their kindness I was careful not to mention, "See you soon in Angleterre!"

(Royal Festival Hall — London — 1989)

The concert tour was a roller coaster and not without unforeseen problems.

The first trumpet cut her lip and chipped a tooth whilst diving into a swimming pool. Of course, I was blamed for it by the conductor.

My son Oliver developed a nasty rash on his lips and tongue and all I could do was to offer him a straw so that he could at least have drinks.

One morning, when we were all on the buses and ready to leave le Lude, where we were staying with families, we found that two boys were missing and when I looked at the accommodation list I remembered that they had had the privilege of staying in the local chateau. I sent two teachers to fetch them. They returned very distressed and told me that the huge gates were locked and nobody would answer the bell. "Leave it to me," I reassured them.

The night before I had been given a security code for the gates by the count himself, which he had programmed to the date of birth of our Queen Elizabeth as appreciation for her inviting him to visit her at Buckingham Palace. But I just couldn't remember her date of birth. After a long discussion, two parents put their heads together and worked out her birthdate. We rushed back to the gate and entered the number into a side panel. Lo and behold, the grand gates opened for us, but nobody was to be seen. To our surprise the main door of the chateau was unlocked. We rushed from one stately room to another and eventually found the two boys fast asleep in a four-poster bed in a room on the second floor!

After the great success of the French concert tour, the Surrey County Youth Orchestra's committee decided to travel to Germany in two years' time. Again all heads were turned towards me. Since my youngest son, Oliver, was still a member of the orchestra, I weakened.

Whenever the Surrey Youth Orchestra gave a concert they always invited the winner of the BBC Musician of the Year, which was a great inspiration for all the young musicians. When we toured in France our soloist was Caroline Dearnley, a promising young cellist, who excelled herself when playing the Elgar Cello Concerto. The conductor was Christopher Adey. Every time the orchestra played Tchaikovsky's Francesca da Rimini, they brought the house down and they had to give sometimes more than one encore. When we performed in Germany we travelled with the talented soloist Emma-Jane Murphy who played the Saint-Saens Cello Concerto in A minor, under the baton of John Forster.

Again the German Rhineland tour was hard work but a very rewarding experience.

53. A CHANGE OF ROLES

An opportunity lent itself to me to switch support roles.

Frank had always been keen on politics but felt disappointed with the Labour Party he had supported for many years. When a new party, the SDP (Social Democratic Party) came to a new political horizon, he felt very passionate about it and became a founder member.

The first meeting took place in our living room and, although I am not a political animal, I tried my best to take on the role of a good hostess, serving apple strudel with whipped cream (I used the secret recipe of my mother which included soaking the apples in Austrian 80% Inland Stroh rum).

This meeting was followed by numerous fundraising barbecues in aid of the SDP in our garden, where we provided food and drink to over fifty members with Frank being the 'head barbecuer' and me providing salads, Black Forest gateaux and various other Austrian cakes. We met (the ever so handsome!) Dr David Owen and Roy Jenkins and we nominated Margaret Sharp as our MP.

After some years of hard work and with the enthusiasm of its members, the SDP was merged with the Liberal Party and became Lib Dem.

Frank, however, decided to abandon his political pursuits and took up serious jogging. We were all so proud of him when he completed the London and Paris marathons in aid of Save the Children.

During this time Frank had another career change. He was offered the position of chief solicitor for Nationwide. As always, being the caring person he was, he became an agony aunt to his staff. He believed in my dowsing skills and very often would phone me to 'link in' on a member of his staff who suffered from depression or emotional upheavals to find the appropriate Bach remedy. He also learned from me how to relieve headaches using acupressure points.

Frank was voted to be the chairman of the Holborn Law Society's International Committee. This entailed privileges, such as travels abroad (with accompanying wife – me!) and also an invitation to the Queen's garden party, where I was hoping to meet up with a close relative of the Queen, whom I had treated – and I was lucky!

54. FROM MUSIC TO THERAPY

In the strange way that fate conducts itself, it was through my involvement with music that I discovered the path that was to lead to my work as a natural health practitioner and eventually to establish my natural health clinic in Guildford.

In fact it would be true to say that I embarked upon my new career feet first! It was after a lesson with a young gifted violinist that I confided to her mother that my neck and shoulder were causing me such discomfort that I was considering giving up teaching the violin. To my surprise she became very excited and asked if I had thought of trying reflexology, which she had learned recently whilst in Germany. I was very sceptical that a treatment of the feet could have any bearing on my problem and politely dismissed the idea but she insisted on allowing her to try as she had made a study of this form of therapy and thought it might help. I reluctantly surrendered my foot.

My friend, Bérangère, started to apply pressure at various points on my feet. I had imagined that it would be little more than a pleasurable massage but to my surprise, or perhaps shock would be more accurate, I experienced great discomfort and intense stabs of pain from certain pressure manipulations. This was no fun and I was very relieved when the session was over and congratulated myself that I had at least given it a try. I thought no more about it until a few days later when getting dressed, Frank expressed surprise that I had managed to do up my bra without his assistance. It was true. My shoulder had regained more movement and I did not experience so much pain. This was a remarkable outcome given the many years I had suffered with this problem. Clearly, whatever my earlier misgivings, this form of therapy was worthy of further study and I set about finding courses that would be available to me.

I phoned various hospitals and was referred to different departments from psychiatry to neurology but reflexology as a recognised therapy remained something of an 'oddball'. Finally, by good fortune, I spoke to the receptionist at St Mary's Hospital in London who knew that her matron was going to take part in the first teachings in reflexology of the International Institute of Reflexology in London and she kindly provided a contact number for me to follow up.

I was so excited and managed to get enrolled. I found this new approach to hands-on healing so amazing and decided to complete the course.

Eventually, I graduated with a diploma in reflexology. I was now a fully-fledged reflexologist.

55. SEARCH FOR KNOWLEDGE

Having experienced the proof of the pudding and continued with my own study of reflexology I resolved to find out more about the world of natural medicine and healing. I visited the first health exhibition held at Olympia in London in 1983 and I was amazed at the wealth of natural healing therapies on show and the large number of people attending the exhibition. I was spoilt for choice but I was especially attracted to the section concerned with iridology (the study of health conditions reflected in the iris) which made a lot of sense to me as I had always felt, even as a child, that the eyes were an indicator of health – both physical and emotional. As a consequence I enrolled in a two-year intensive course in iridology and naturopathy at Cambridge working with an inspiring teacher called Farida Sharon who used to fly in from California to instruct us.

It was from Farida that I learnt of some other impressive work being undertaken in Colombo by Sir Anton Jayasuriya, an eminent professor attached to the South General Hospital in Kalubowila. He had created an annex to the hospital for the teaching and treatments of acupuncture, the principles of homoeopathy, and manipulative medicines. Farida had obtained an honourable doctorate in natural medicine under his tutelage and I became ambitious to achieve the same.

To do so meant leaving my family for the duration of the course, a period of three months. Frank, as always, was very encouraging and assured me that he was more than capable of spoiling the children and our two dogs in my absence and that the whole family would be very proud to have a 'barefoot doctor' in the house.

And so I went to Sri Lanka and immersed myself in a comprehensive study of natural health therapies under the guidance of Professor Anton, author of over twenty publications, such as 'Clinical Homoeopathy' and a nine-hundred page synopsis, a masterpiece on clinical acupuncture, which serves for teaching courses and for reference.

56. COLOMBO, SRI LANKA

In Colombo we worked a six-day week, from eight in the morning until two in the afternoon with lessons on clinical applications given by Professor Anton. Later in the evening we observed practical demonstrations of acupuncture and practised needle insertion into the bark of a tree. Once we had passed the test we were allowed to treat patients under the careful supervision of his qualified staff. There were at least 150 patients to be seen every day.

There was no burdensome administration needed. New patients would queue in the morning to see the professor and after assessment, he marked details of the patient and prognosis on a card for us and they were asked to bring the card back with them on each visit. Patients were treated outside, sitting on chairs or lying on wooden benches in the shade of the trees.

It was an amazing sight to see beautiful ladies in their colourful saris with immaculately brushed hair, children and babies, men, amputees and drug addicts. There were also patients who had travelled from abroad to receive treatment. Not all the patients spoke English and I was concerned that I was having less success with the native, non-English-speaking patients. Whenever they returned I would ask them if they felt there was any improvement after my having treated them. They shook their heads in a circular motion, which I took to be a negative response. Later, when consulting with one of the resident doctors I learned that the mannerism of shaking their heads as they had done meant yes. I was greatly relieved and encouraged.

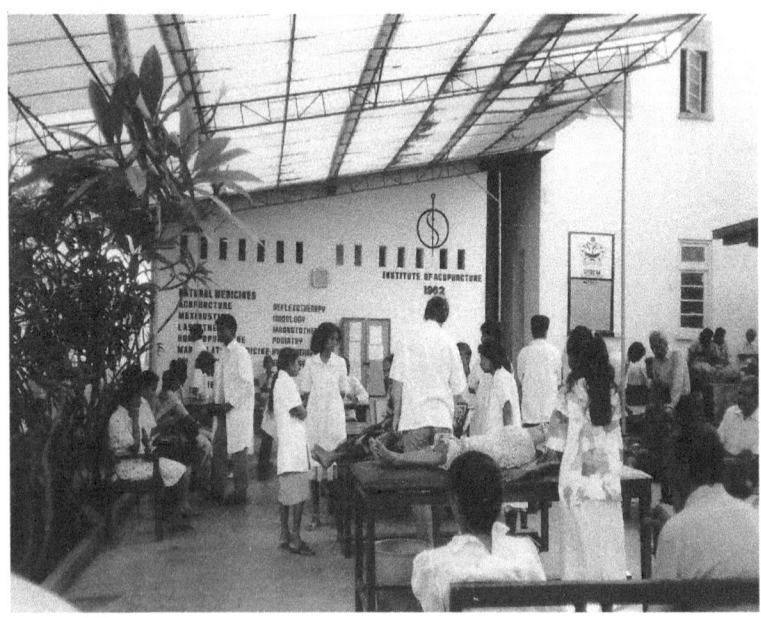

During my time at the hospital we were shown a number of films where, during surgery, the methodology of acupuncture was truly amazing. I witnessed cases of acute bronchial asthma restored to normal breathing after only ten to fifteen minutes; a lady being operated on during acupuncture anaesthesia for a huge growth on her neck, sipping tea during the operation; and cases of long-standing frozen shoulders restored to improved mobility after just a few sessions. The whole experience was both enlightening and truly inspiring.

To apply for a doctorate in natural medicine one had to be fully qualified in anatomy, physiology and pathology, three major natural health therapies, and to pass a number of written exam papers and oral exams. Acupuncture was one of the requirements, which I managed to complete. My certificate of iridology and naturopathy was also accepted. Reflexology didn't count and, since kinesiology was a lesser-known therapy at that time, I was asked to submit a thesis, which took me one year to complete. After this I received my MD (MA).

Maya Kraus

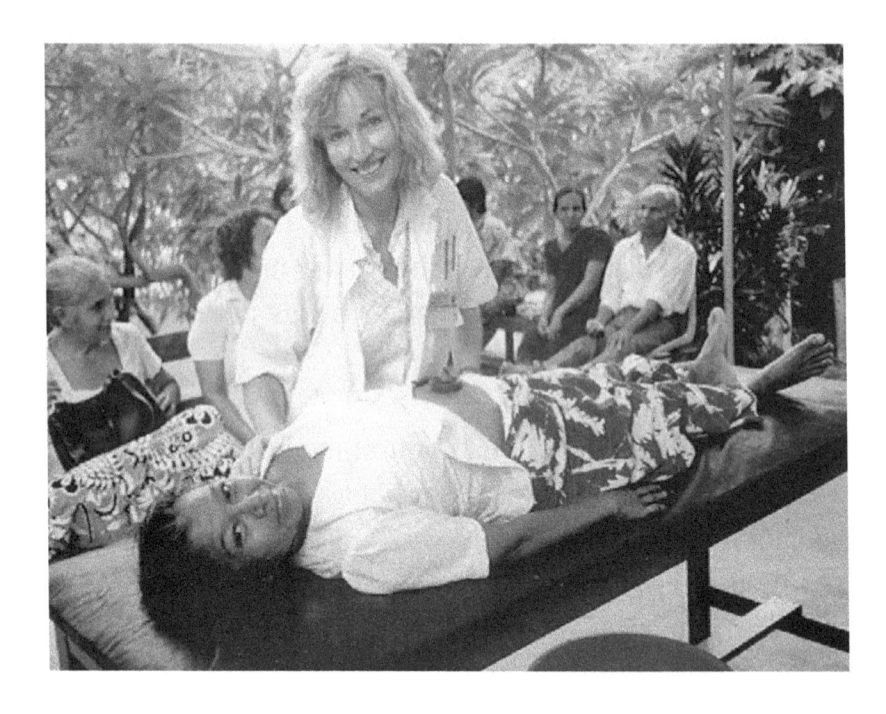

57. TOUCH FOR HEALTH

There was another area of healthcare that interested me, called applied kinesiology, involving an understanding of the muscles of the body and the way weaknesses and imbalances can be identified via a specific muscle-testing procedure. Once a weak muscle is identified, the muscle can then be strengthened with the help of acupuncture points and other specific points on the body or the head.

I think my attraction to this can be attributed to my childhood when I experienced considerable discomfort from a neck injury at the age of eleven which remained with me for many years and made movement difficult (even though I managed to become the winner of the regional schools' sports event whilst at my grammar school in Stuttgart at the age of fourteen). At first I was sceptical, as, indeed, I had been when introduced to reflexology, but because of that experience, I opened my mind to its possibilities and enrolled for a course of kinesiology with Ann Holdway, called Touch for Health. It proved to be a very valuable tool in my practice.

As my knowledge and experience developed, so my reputation as a healer grew among my friends and relatives and, inevitably, in time the circle widened as referrals were initiated until I found myself overwhelmed by demand.

I made no charge or sometimes only a nominal fee for my services (which no doubt explained my popularity) but I was rewarded with a houseful of beautiful flowers and an overflowing supply of expensive chocolates.

At this time I was using my Surrey home as the base for treatments but such was the traffic of clients and the congestion they brought to this quiet hamlet that the neighbours, quite understandably, voiced their complaints. The arrival of a helicopter on the village green carrying a VIP to see me for treatment proved to be the last straw and it was clear that something had to be done!

58. CASTLE STREET CLINIC

After many months of searching and exhausting the patience of local estate agents, we eventually found a property in the heart of Guildford overlooking the historic castle grounds. The ground floor was a French restaurant business called Café de Paris and a kitchen shop, Intoto, and both paid rent for their occupancy. On the second level the building had previously housed the offices of an insurance and solicitor's business and it offered the right kind of space and ambience for our new venture to create eight therapy rooms, office, kitchen, reception and waiting area.

Unfortunately, our own bank was less than helpful when it came to providing a mortgage to purchase the property, but we eventually found an alternative bank with a young enterprising manager (a man of vision) who agreed to provide us with a generous loan. He calculated that the rent from the restaurant and the kitchen shop together with other sources of income from letting therapy rooms and our private stake would enable us to buy the property.

I could now work in a multi-disciplinary environment to enable me to develop my work further and to engage other practitioners offering different therapies.

At the same time I had the sneaky suspicion that Frank's enthusiasm to purchase the property had a great deal to do with the restaurant, reflecting his love of all things French, especially fine cuisine.

We had a formal opening ceremony by the mayor of Guildford and this is how, in 1994, Castle Street Clinic was born and happily it continues to serve the community today.

When in the year 2000, Thierry, the owner of the restaurant decided to retire, Frank seized the opportunity to become the new patron. He put his heart and soul into the business, studying the art of cuisine with a passion in order to gain the respect of his new colleagues. He even took part in a one-year cookery course at La Tante Marie. The reputation of the restaurant rose considerably under his directorship, achieving an entry in the Michelin Guide and the award of two AA rosettes.

Traditional French Brasserie & Restaurant

59. THE HEALING YEARS

One night whilst playing as a co-leader of an operatic society I became aware that my leader was experiencing some discomfort and during a break in which the soprano performed her libretto, I whispered to her to ask what the problem was. "My neck is killing me," she mumbled.

I indicated to her to give me her left hand and I quickly worked the reflex points for neck and shoulder. She looked at me quizzically. "It's not my hand, it's my neck!" she exclaimed. There was no time to explain. The cue came to continue playing which we did with gusto.

After the performance she asked me what I had done that had been so effective in curing the pain she had experienced. I explained how reflexology is based on a ten-zone system and that the area from the thumb towards the wrist is related to neck and back problems. She was very impressed and soon after she referred her sister and a musician friend to me to receive treatment for shoulder and back problems. This led to many other referrals and earned me the name of 'musician's friend'.

A musician friend of mine referred a fellow musician to come and see me. She was due to give a solo performance at the Royal Festival Hall in London but was suffering from severe sciatica. The previous year she had had to cancel her concert due to the same problem.

Although she had received traction, which was very painful, it took her many months to recover. Her doctor had recommended that she repeat the treatment but she was reluctant to put herself through the ordeal. I gave her reflexology and Chinese acupressure massage which alleviated much of her pain.

On a follow-up visit she still expressed concern as to whether she would be able to perform. She explained that although much of the pain she had experienced before had subsided she was sometimes caught unawares by a sharp pain in her back radiating down her leg which made her feel paralysed. The last thing she wanted to do was walk on the stage with a walking stick!

I thought of kinesiology and explained to her that I was going to apply a procedure called touch for health and reassured her that it would not cause any discomfort.

During muscle testing I came across a weak muscle on her left foot called the peroneus. I made the necessary corrections and explained that this muscle is prone to ankle and foot problems. I asked her if she had ever suffered from an ankle injury. She replied that as far as she could remember there had never been a problem.

The following day I received a phone call from her to say that she had remembered seriously injuring her ankle playing rounders at school when she was twelve years old.

The story has a happy ending. I was told that she managed to play her concerto without any discomfort and a little later I received a postcard from her, thanking me for my help and informing me that she was on a walking holiday in the Himalayas and was fully recovered.

Maya Kraus

60. SUCCESS AND FAILURE

As a consequence of the work undertaken at my home, I was invited by the local cancer support group to join the members and to offer what help I could. The meetings took the form of a friendly and relaxed gathering in which participants could talk about their situation and share their experiences in a supportive ambience.

On one occasion an elderly and frail gentleman, who suffered from prostate cancer, reported to the group that after receiving treatment from me he had managed to control his bladder much better and that he had managed to drive up north to visit his sick brother without needing the toilet. He had not been able to achieve this before because at that time there were no disabled toilet facilities at the petrol stations on the way. It was heartening news and the group was uplifted by the story.

When the meeting concluded one of the supporters, a local doctor, approached me and asked if she could see me at her home. I readily agreed and imagined that the invitation was in connection with her daughter whom I knew was suffering from a condition known as viral fatigue syndrome or now more commonly referred to as ME or 'yuppie flu'. I arrived fully equipped with books on reflexology, kinesiology and recent case histories of patients whom I had helped.

The doctor led me to an attractively decorated sitting room with large windows that provided good light and a generous view of the garden. On the way, we passed a small box room in which I briefly observed the daughter sitting up in bed watching the television, which had been placed at the end of her bed. The curtains were drawn so that the room had a gloomy feel as though the daughter had been placed in some kind of detention.

I asked the doctor if this was the daughter she was concerned about and she confirmed that it was but stated "that she didn't want to see visitors". No sooner had we arrived in the sitting room and with no invitation to place my books down, the doctor turned towards me in a hostile fashion and in a sharp tone asked, "So, tell me about kinesiology and what is so special about it?"

I was taken aback but I gave her a brief account of how muscle testing works and how it is possible to access the body to discover weaknesses, allergies and so forth. I then ventured to interest her in the emotional aspect of kinesiology and mentioned that it can prove beneficial in working with hidden stressors and embrace sensory cognitive issues.

At this point she fixed me with cold eyes and snapped aggressively: "So tell me what cognitive means!"

I was shocked and completely thrown off balance by her manner which amounted to verbal violence and to my embarrassment and regret I burst out in tears. "You see, you don't even know what you are talking about. You are a danger to patients!" She handed me a large man-sized box of tissues with triumphant disdain.

It was time to leave. I recovered my equilibrium and wanted to address her directly and say: "At a recent meeting you shared with the group how concerned you were that your daughter is suffering from ill health and has been bedridden for many months. I came to your house as an invited guest full of goodwill in the hope that I might be of some help. I have been extremely hurt by your attitude and lack of respect and very much regret that, due to your prejudice, your daughter is not to be given the opportunity to receive a therapy that certainly would not do any harm and might well be beneficial."

My throat had completely closed up and I had totally lost my voice and had to resort to a quiet mental reply instead. I felt much better for having stood my corner, silently, although I was never invited back again to the cancer support group. The imprisonment of that unfortunate young girl in her dark room when there was a more cheerful and positive environment readily available saddened me but there was nothing I could do.

Maya Kraus

61. ITAPARICA, BRAZIL

One day Frank came home with a collection of holiday brochures and asked me to choose the ideal holiday. I browsed through the many brochures and homed in, with my dowsing skills, on a Club Med holiday resort in the north of Brazil called Itaparica. When we arrived, Frank was very disappointed because there was no opportunity for diving or jogging, both of which were pleasures for him. The area where we were situated was on a small estate and completely enclosed. Even the beach was guarded by police. It was not a very promising situation. I remembered a poem given to me by my friend, Jeanette, a psychic healer, who said I should refer to it when I arrived at Itaparica.

The poem was related to an ancient saying of a Canadian Indian and it read:

>Tall Trees
>Warm Fire
>Strong Wind
>Deep Water
>I feel you in my body
>I feel you in my soul.

I looked up at the trees and sure enough they were very tall.

It was extremely hot, the sea was deep blue and there was a constant cooling breeze. I just laughed in amazement.

On the third evening before our departure Frank and I went for a stroll when all of a sudden, as if from nowhere, a cyclist appeared at full speed around a bend. He managed to stop by breaking and raising the front wheel up like a horse rearing up on two hind legs. The rider apologised in French (at last someone we could understand) and he introduced himself as Jeromico.

He invited us to be his guests and attend a show at a circus the next day where he was to perform as a trapeze artist. Sadly, he told us, his partner, Flavia, was not able to participate because of an injury on her left leg. Having been offered the free tickets I suggested that maybe I could do something to help as a way of responding to his generosity and I explained about reflexology.

He was very interested and open to its possibilities and that evening he arrived at our accommodation with Flavia sitting on the handlebar of his bike. The main area of trauma was on her foot which was very painful and she was resistant to having it touched. I assured her that I would not cause her any discomfort and I began by holding my hands a few inches away from around her foot. Eventually I was able to touch her foot without complaint.

My hands guided me to an area on the plantar of her foot and to my amazement as I continued working, I found various colours appear from a dark purple to shades of green and yellow under my hands. I stroked the colours away with swift movements and to the astonishment of Frank and Jeromico (and to me also it must be said) the foot took on a healthy complexion and the pain Flavia had experienced eased considerably so that I was able to touch her foot and massage various reflex points.

The next evening Frank and I were given front row seats by Jeromico to watch the circus show and I was quite shocked to see Flavia climb up a rope to the small platform in the roof of the tent and then start to swing on a trapeze, holding on with just her injured foot. I could hardly bear to look and to make matters worse there was no safety net! I felt relieved when the act was over and joined in the rapturous applause. At that point Jeromico and Flavia approached me and taking me by the hand they led me to the centre of the ring and told the audience about the 'miraculous treatment' I had given her. They then presented me with a huge bouquet of exotic flowers and invited me to return the following day at three o'clock so that they could teach me how to fly the trapeze.

They were not to know of my childhood dream of joining the circus and just how thrilled I was to have the opportunity to take part again.

Unfortunately, that very evening I developed a nasty cough and a chest infection, which ruled out any chance of flying the trapeze and I had to content myself by watching Frank undergo a lesson under the careful instruction of Jeromico. I admit to being more than a little jealous but I was also very proud of the bravery Frank displayed in climbing the rope ladder to the small platform and then swinging to and fro mid-air on a trapeze before letting go and landing somewhat inelegantly into the safety net. I was amazed at the grey mucous I produced. On the way to the airport the taxi driver decided to stop off at a pharmacy and bought me a cough mixture.

What was this all about? – I realised then that I managed to release my suppressed grief after a neck injury all those years ago when I had to abandon my greatest ambition – to become a trapeze artist.

The poem my healer friend Jeanette gave me enabled me to 'feel in my body'!

Sometimes, when I treated a sports injury or worked on a painful area, colours would appear during my healing and in many cases the person recovered very quickly.

I remember seeing an attractive lady who was very distressed. She was a keen tennis player but had injured her knee.

I placed two crystals at specific places on her knee and began to use my hands. Within a few minutes we both noticed various colours appear around her injury, which I gently stroked away.

After the treatment she could bend her knee and walk away with less pain. One week later, she recommended a friend of hers who seemed to suffer with similar problems. The lady arrived and, without asking me, she entered my therapy room, accompanied by her husband, her two daughters and two friends.

I didn't have enough chairs and my therapy room was overcrowded. They came with great excitement and anticipation to witness a spectacle. However, muscle testing indicated a referral to her GP or chiropractor for further investigation and scans. They left disappointed and felt cheated. Later on I learned that she had to have an operation on her knee which was successful.

Maya Kraus

62. OUT OF BODY

I was admitted to Queen Anne's Hospital to undergo a gynaecological operation for a condition known as a blocked Bartholin gland. It was a straightforward operation but required specialist knowledge. After the procedure was completed and I was in recovery there was a complication. Blood was escaping from below and it could not be stemmed. There was great concern from the hospital staff as the situation was life-threatening and urgent. My specialist was sent for and he was rushed to the hospital under police escort. So serious was the situation that Frank, who was on business in Leeds, was contacted and advised to come immediately to the hospital.

After some difficulty administering the needle for a blood transfusion for severe blood loss, I was placed under anaesthesia and here I experienced a phenomenon that I had read about and heard about from others which was referred to as an out-of-body experience. I was looking directly down at myself on the operating table and I could see the operation being conducted as clear as could be. I was aware of the surgeon and his medical team around him. I was even able to witness a conversation bordering on flirtation by two theatre assistants and actually became vexed by their seeming casualness to the drama being played out. All of a sudden there was an injection of urgency on the part of the theatre team.

I could hear the words "We are losing her". There was a great deal of activity around my body and I was aware of a doctor pumping my chest so aggressively in fact that this caused a hairline crack in my shoulder, as it was later confirmed on X-ray. Yet none of this caused me any distress. I was in a state of complete calm. It was the most amazing experience. It seemed to me that I was bathed in a bright, heavenly light and was moving slowly through a tunnel. If this was death then I had no fear of it. But I did care for my children and my husband and I wanted desperately to live for them. I held pictures of them in my mind's eye and reached out to them. Gradually the light softened and then darkness.

The next thing I remembered was seeing the face of a nurse looking into my face and smiling. At first I was uncertain where I was but soon realised that I was in a bed in a hospital ward. The nurse informed me that I had given the medical staff something of a scare and added that at one point I had been declared clinically dead. "It is a miracle that you are alive," she said. For my part I cannot explain what the experience was. I can only say that it happened and that it convinced me that there are dimensions to human existence that cannot be comprehended by the rational mind.

On thinking back, I now realise that my own vanity had caused this complication.

Before the operation of the Bartholin gland my gynaecologist recommended having a sterilisation which he could perform at the same time since my womb seemed to be 'raw' and not healthy enough for further pregnancies. It meant making a small incision at the navel.

I was very conscious of having regained my figure after three children – and no stretch marks (!) and I did not want any intrusion to scar my body and so I refused. He then recommended that I could try a new method of birth control – the pill. I took his advice and went to my local surgery.

After only having taken one tablet in the evening, I remember walking about the next morning as if a brick had hit my head and I abandoned the pill. I eventually consented to have the sterilisation.

A few days after my major operation, the anaesthetist met my husband and told him that the procedure, a sterilisation from below, was perhaps not the best approach. It had caused a rupture of the womb which had resulted in severe haemorrhaging.

Maya Kraus

63. PSYCHIC OR WHAT?

I have often been asked if I am psychic but I have never claimed it for myself. I prefer to be recognised as a healer using complementary medicine and practices to help people. It is true that I have experienced moments of insights or perceptions from childhood onwards that I cannot explain, but the idea that I have special powers is not something that I entertain comfortably and indeed I have resisted it. I do, however, believe in what I call 'the wisdom of the universe' which has served me well in my work and which is available to everyone if you allow yourself to be receptive to its gift of knowledge.

I also wonder whether the gift of psychic sensitivity can be passed down through generations. My grandfather on my father's side was said to have psychic abilities. There is one particular story told to me about him which is very bizarre.

During the First World War, whilst in the thick of fighting, he pointed out a soldier lying some distance away on the crest of the hill who appeared to be waving in his direction. The order was given to ignore him and to keep moving but my grandfather broke rank and made his way up the hill past many dead soldiers to discover that the soldier waving turned out to be his brother who was severely injured. He picked him up and carried him on his back, making the return journey more hazardous.

Sadly, neither brother survived the war but a soldier friend returned home safely to tell the story to our family.

It took me a year to recover from my major operation, mainly due to my busy life. Family always came first and I was lucky to have had help in the house and kind friends to help out with school runs. I would get up at 5 a.m., place a mute on my violin and practise scales and the work my teacher had set for me. Somehow I managed to keep my jewellery business running – whilst still being addicted to Librium.

Soon after my out of body experience something very strange came about. I started to have violent (psychic?) dreams of accidents the night before they happened. I dreamed about disasters well before they occurred and were reported on the news, e.g. a lightweight aeroplane crashed in the nearby village Bramley and killed two girls travelling in a car.

These dreams were so vivid, they left me utterly exhausted for many hours and when they continued to happen I asked God and the universe to stop them. They stopped.

Something else changed when I started to work as a therapist. I found it more difficult to see the aura as clearly as before.

Instead my body seemed to have become a sensor to my patients' health problems. Whenever I appraised them I would receive an empathetic response.

For example, a patient might come with a sports injury to be treated, but suddenly I would feel a sharp pain on my gums and when questioning the person they would confirm that indeed they had toothache at the same spot that I felt it and I would send them to the dentist. Or I would start to feel a tight sore throat, or a pain in my body during the treatment, pointing to a pressing health issue I was previously unaware of as the patient omitted to mention it when filling in my patient form. The moment this was confirmed by my patients, my own discomfort suddenly disappeared as quickly as it came and I felt normal again – thank goodness!

This is strange to some but a useful diagnostic tool for me, and so far I have never been wrong or harmed in any way. Sometimes, however, the body would not indicate to me a more serious underlying health problem this way and I think this is due to the wisdom of the body not to frighten the person, the stress of which in turn could accelerate a disease.

After treatment I always check with the body to see whether the person could benefit from seeing a conventional doctor or another therapist.

I usually finish the treatment by checking whether testing for supplements, food intolerances, allergies or geopathic stress are important.

I use my dowsing skills or muscle testing to find priority issues to be treated; that way the body and mind cannot become stressed during the treatment and I can safely work in tune with the body's healing energy. I never diagnose.

I also found that sometimes, during my treatments, some of my patients experienced seeing the colours of the chakras I was working on.

Maybe there is a link or 'spark' to pass on healing abilities from one healer to another person. Sometimes my patients were so inspired that they took their own path to studying natural health therapies and ultimately to practise healing.

During my life's journey I had many spiritual experiences and I would like to share some of these with you.

We were travelling on the German motorway to go to my father's funeral. I must have dozed off, when, all of a sudden, I heard the distinguished voice of my father's calling out: 'Pass auf!' (careful). I opened my eyes and, to my shock and horror noticed, that a huge lorry in front of us had started to move into our lane.

I shouted out to Frank and, just in time, he managed to brake hard to avoid a serious accident.

A few months later, one early morning, I woke up and saw that our bedroom was lit by a gentle white light. In front of our wardrobe I saw the clear image of my father. He looked a much younger man and his outlines stopped by his waist. He was smiling at me. Whilst looking at him, I was overcome by a blissful warm feeling of love. It happened at a time when we had serious financial worries and I was very stressed.

My husband had been deceived by his partner. I then knew that I was not alone and that I was supported by the spirit world with love. When I tried to share this experience with my mother, she brushed it away and said that it was a lot of nonsense and that I was only dreaming. There was no point in sharing any further details with her.

Some years later, when my mother was seriously ill in hospital, I tried to comfort her and told her that Papa was with her. "I know," she said, "I have seen him passing by my bed." She had seen the same likeness of my father as I had experienced – that of a younger man, from the waist up and smiling.

It sometimes happens that a spirit makes its presence known to me.

I am always aware of this whenever I feel a gentle, cool wind blowing around my legs, causing me to get goose pimples and, at the same time, there is a very peaceful feeling surrounding me.

A young man I call Charlie came to see me to seek help. He wanted to find out why he was always so angry with everything and everyone, and why he even rejected his parents' love. All of a sudden, my therapy room was filled with a strong smell of paint and oil of turpentine. I opened my window and my door to investigate. The smell was in my therapy room. Then I experienced the usual sensation whenever a spirit presents itself. I asked Charlie, whether he was aware of a certain smell in our room.

He then burst into tears. "It reminds me of my grandfather, who was an artist and with whom I spent many hours in his atelier, watching him paint. When I was eight years old, my grandfather died suddenly of a heart attack, and I was not allowed to come to the funeral. I was told that I was too young," he sobbed. "I was not allowed to say goodbye," he added.

We lit a candle and thanked the spirit. Charlie was able to say his goodbye! This experience changed his life.

64. RAYNAUD'S SYNDROME

Not very long after my major operation I noticed that my hands and especially my fingers were always cold and sometimes turned white. On many occasions, when shopping in a supermarket, even on a hot day, I lost all feeling in my hands and I had to ask the check-out assistant to take the money out of my purse. No matter whether I wore gloves before entering a supermarket, my hands and fingers became numb.

This condition was a serious handicap for a musician who played the violin. I often resorted to bathing my hands in warm water to restore the feeling and dexterity before each rehearsal and concert. Usually there were toilet facilities available but, as a precaution, I used to equip myself with a thermos flask of hot water and a teabag to serve as a plug for the washbasin should it be necessary.

My doctor diagnosed this condition as Raynaud's syndrome and told me that it was a vasospastic disorder and that there was no cure.

In my own mind I put the condition down to a trauma or body shock that I had experienced during my resuscitation. Later on, whilst studying health kinesiology, I explored the idea that some kind of mental blockage inhibiting my circulation might be the cause of the problem.

Together with my teacher we worked on this idea with the result that the condition improved dramatically. I wrote a long letter to the Raynaud's & Scleroderma Association explaining my story but unfortunately I never heard back from them.

65. YUGOSLAVIA

During my stay in Colombo, I met some doctors who were very interested in my work. They invited me to take part in their first International Congress of Alternative Medicine in Belgrade and to give a series of lectures to doctors in kinesiology and iridology. I accepted their invitation and was overwhelmed by the response my lectures received. I was even invited to take part in a radio programme and I made several appearances on different television channels. On one occasion I was on prime-time television following the six o'clock news. The presenter introduced me as a "healer from England" and invited me to check his irises.

Apart from various stress rings and a knee injury, both of which he acknowledged, I found that his right kidney was congested and showed alarming disease signs causing some distress to his lower back. Having been warned that the presenter was a personality much loved by the viewers I cautiously asked him whether he had ever experienced any back pain to which he replied: "No, I never have back pain."

I pressed him a little more firmly and he responded light-heartedly: "Doesn't everybody have back pain from time to time?" I knew he was being guarded but I didn't pursue it further.

After the show he approached me and confirmed that he did suffer severe back pain and had been treated for urinary and kidney infections on more than one occasion.

The congress was so successful, with every lecture attended by over fifty doctors that the director of the Acupuncture Clinic in Belgrade, Dr. Edwin Dervishevic, organised another conference in the spring of the following year in Sarajevo. I was invited as a guest speaker and was asked to tutor doctors in applied kinesiology. I arrived with flip charts and photocopies but to my amazement I found that every doctor had been given a Touch for Health manual (the basis of kinesiology) translated into Serbo-Croat.

Once again I was invited to appear on radio and television. During a phone-in programme a distraught father called in and asked if I could explain why his young daughter always recovered in hospital yet fell ill again as soon as she was allowed home. I asked him for his daughter's name and then searched quietly in my head. I was 'given' geopathic stress as the cause but was uncertain whether this would be understood.

My translator, a doctor, assured me that he was very aware of the problem and added that it was a well-known farmers' saying that, "If one wants to build a house, one should observe the sheep and where they lie down to sleep it is safe to build".

Every time I came out of the lecture theatre people crowded around me and wanted me to check their irises. It was very demanding and impossible to give my attention to all these people but there was one approach made that I remember especially.

A young man pleaded with me to see his young wife who was a promising university student but was suffering from some kind of paralysis. I attended her in a private room which had been made available to us. She had received hospital treatment over a period of a month but had been discharged without any improvement to her condition. I began by scanning her aura but could find no specific ill-health problems. While scanning her I had a vision of a car accident and when I asked the husband about the possibility, he confirmed that his wife had been involved in a car accident but that she had not suffered any injuries. He did indicate, however, that her problem originated from that time.

This made sense to me and the situation suggested that 'body position memory correction' (a technique I had learned at one of the many seminars I had attended in health kinesiology) would be beneficial.

The procedure involved putting the patient into the position she was in at the time of impact of the accident and employing acupuncture pressure points to specific areas of the body, all guided by muscle testing. I organised the procedure and, all of a sudden, the patient's body jumped up about two inches with a force that shook me and the doctors who were needed to assist me in holding the many acupuncture points required.

This was followed by a period of complete calm. There was nothing else I could do and so returned to my hotel. The following day, after finishing a lecture, I became aware of a young lady approaching me with a huge bunch of gladioli which she handed to me. It was the young wife I had treated the day before. She faced the assembled doctors and told them the story of what had happened the previous day and we both received a prolonged round of applause.

Some weeks later after returning home I received a postcard from her saying:

> 'We always remember, first of September'.

66. THAT'S SHOW BUSINESS

One day Frank came home and told me that a school friend of his, Jonathan Cohen, was going to perform with his 10-strong singing group at Hammersmith. My children and I often watched Playaway on television where Jonathan was on the piano. I was totally swept off my feet by this lively and fun performance. I so wanted to be part of it and I asked Frank to introduce me to Jonathan after the concert.

This is how I became a member of the Corporation, a name given by their sponsors, the Co-operative Society. Frank, as usual, was very supportive when we gave concerts or went on tour, once even to Hungary. We also made an LP and a single, sponsored by Decca Records.

To be in a recording studio was just awesome and very exciting. Our circle of friends increased in different directions. I met Rick Jones, who always delighted our children when they watched him on television as the 'Fingerbob Man'. He told me that he was writing a song for me called: Maya, fly higher. He died unexpectedly before completing it.

One of the singers of the Corporation was Christoph Götting, a violin maker, who studied in Mittenwald in Germany. We instantly bonded and became family friends.

He developed his experience in violin making and restoration in the workshop above the well-known shop 'Beares' in Wardour Street. He was researching the varnish used on famous old violins. Although he used seasoned wood for making new violins, he felt that part of the secret of a truly beautiful sound was due to the varnish applied at the time. He went to Art Galleries to research old master paintings in order to learn about the ancient varnish surfaces.

He offered one of his violins to me at a bargain price with the request to 'play it in'. He asked me if I would allow him to borrow the violin from time to time in order to appraise his formula. After many years of research, he feels that he has now mastered an exceptional sound and his instruments became so renowned that even the leader of the Berlin Philharmonic bought a violin from him.

On one occasion, when I visited him at the workshop to get my violin bow re-haired, he indicated for me to look at a violin case which was on his bench and asked me to open it. I was amazed.

All I could see were pieces of wood in various sizes like a jigsaw puzzle. These were the remains of an Amati that had been sold to a Japanese violinist who lived in Paris. When visiting London she attempted to cross the road but unfortunately she looked the wrong way.

She just managed to jump out of the way of a passing car but her violin case got hit and thrown into the road. Now Christoph had the most challenging task to carry out its restoration! I couldn't believe that it would be possible but Christoph assured me that, although it would be difficult and take some time, it would be as good as new.

The sad incident of the violin accident took me back to my first experience, when I tried to use the London Bus Services. There was a queue at the bus stop and, having learned at school in Germany that English people are polite, I joined the waiting travellers at the back. The bus arrived from the opposite direction I wanted to travel and I suddenly realized why the people waiting gave me hostile looks – I had stood at the front of the queue!

I felt very embarrassed and quickly crossed the road to wait at the other bus stop. I could see the bus arriving but it didn't stop! The next bus passed by and the same thing happened again. Luckily an old lady joined me and when I explained to her what had happened, she laughed and pointed at a red sign, indicating it was a request bus stop and I should signal my intention by raising my arm. When the next bus approached I waved my arm frantically and lo and behold - it stopped.

Maya Kraus

67. FREEDOM FROM LIBRIUM

As had happened so many times in my life, it was a chance meeting that set me off on a new path. I was accompanying my son Oliver to a music lesson. The teacher, Miss Band, was an honourable member of the Royal Academy of Music. She was a sprightly lady of eighty years young and had a novel approach to her teaching. She would dance around the room with Oli before commencing the lesson: "How can he play the waltz, if he is unable to dance and feel the music?" she would say.

During one of these sessions she commented that I did not look very well and indeed I was feeling exhausted and finding it hard to concentrate. I explained how the Librium caused me to feel drowsy and she recommended that I arrange an appointment with a Dr Latto, a homoeopathic doctor, who was based in Reading and who she felt would be able to help.

Dr Latto was a charming, distinguished man of mature years, who listened very patiently to my story and asked me many questions about myself and my lifestyle. How refreshing it was to have someone in the medical profession able to give so much time to a patient and be so understanding. I made several visits afterwards and always it was the same unhurried approach and sympathetic ear.

He gave me some sound advice about how to manage my life with an emphasis on relaxation and good diet.

"No dead hens, coffee and no sugar or chocolate – you are sweet enough."

Within a very short period of time I stopped taking the Librium and I began to feel much more in control of my life and much happier. I also learnt a very good lesson about giving patients time and about listening patiently and sympathetically which I consider very important in my own approach to my work.

68. WHAT OF EDI?

The last time I saw Edi was on a visit to see my parents in Leinfelden. I found myself standing on a square, surrounded by a newly built shopping complex – the very spot where once a hut was erected to house refugees which included my family. On my left the railway track was long gone and the embankment where Edi and I spend many happy hours running up and down to pick wild strawberries and where I once found a four-leaved clover was now levelled out and landscaped. I watched the busy shoppers hurrying past, unaware that they were walking over the area where so many had once suffered sadness, grief, hunger and despair.

My daughter Pamela was now three years old and the same age as when my family arrived in Leinfelden with two suitcases which contained our only possessions. Lost in the memories which surfaced, both with good times with Edi and the sad times of war, I was sharply brought back to reality by Pamela, who pulled me by the hand wanting to move on.

And then it happened. Suddenly in the midst of all the shoppers there stood Edi. It was like an electric shock and I wondered for a moment if my imagination had somehow conjured him up. But no, this was certainly Edi, now a tall, strapping young man.

His face had lost its boyishness but there was no mistaking him. This was my childhood sole mate. We recognised each other immediately but we were unprepared. Both of us felt awkward and even a little embarrassed. We had enjoyed such a lot of adventures and fun together as children and had been so much at ease with each other but a great deal of water had passed under the bridge since those days. He still had a gap in his teeth and a slight lisp and his eyes were as sparkly as I remembered and there was still a wonderful casualness about his dress, which contrasted with my own attention to fashion.

I think I was the first to speak but I can't be sure. We exchanged potted accounts of ourselves in a formal way. He was a builder, "making out all right", as he put it, and I was genuinely reassured to hear it. He listened to my story and nodded politely from time to time and asked a few questions. The problem was that in telling our respective stories we were reinforcing the distance between us.

When we parted I felt an overwhelming mixture of emotions. I was pleased that we had met and happy that life had treated him kindly but suddenly I missed him terribly.

Why had we carefully avoided intimacy? He had been my best friend. Why hadn't I put my arms around him and told him that I missed him.

I looked in the direction in which he had left in the hope of seeing him and perhaps catching up with him but he was gone.

Maya Kraus

69. A SAD TIME

The death of Frank from bowel cancer at the age of sixty-four was a painful experience for all the family. By the time the problem was confirmed, the cancer had spread and we lived with the knowledge that there was no hope. It was a very difficult time and yet it was also a loving time. Frank displayed remarkable courage and his only concern was for the welfare of his wife and children and, despite a lot of discomfort and pain, he remained cheerful even though it must have been very hard for him.

At his funeral service, in which his life was celebrated, so many people turned up to express their condolences and respect that many had to stand outside the crematorium. It was heart-warming and comforting to witness how many people had been touched by his warmth, generosity and good humour.

Each member of the family found their own way to cope with their grief. Pamela, who is a very spiritual person, spent many hours meditating in a Zen garden that I had created in a quiet corner of the garden. Simon immersed himself in the preparations for the funeral and the programme for the celebration of Frank's life and Oliver composed a moving piece of music which he played on his cello with a photograph of Frank placed on the music stand in front of him.

Some months later I made the decision to visit Chamonix in France, a place where we had enjoyed so many happy family holidays together. I was hoping that in the solitude of the mountains I would find comfort and the strength to face the future without Frank.

I set off early from my hotel and after a five-hour walk and a tricky climb to a high point on the mountain I sat down and watched the dragging clouds above. When I looked down at my feet I noticed to my surprise a stone covered in moss bearing tiny white specks of flowers. It was the only vegetation around in a place where nothing seemed to grow. I felt overcome with a feeling of intense happiness - even in this seemingly barren place there was life and it was beautiful.

I reflected on our life together and began to treasure all the wonderful experiences we had shared. We had certainly had our share of challenges, particularly in the early years of our marriage when Frank was studying and I was coping with work and family, but we had overcome them thanks largely to Frank's indomitable optimism. We had grown stronger in our love for each other. I realised that love overcomes death and that despite the painful loss, I had to trust myself and move on to the challenges ahead in the certain knowledge that Frank's love was, and remains, ever present.

70. NOT THE END

Writing this book has been an emotional journey for me, sometimes raising painful memories and challenging times, but there have been great joys also. I think now that I understand myself better even if the wider question of the mystery of life remains just that.

Is there a predetermined life plan set out for us? Is it all chance? Can I explain the gift I have been blessed with?

The answer is not to be known. I believe that everyone has 'gifts' although not always the good fortune to realise them. I am content to know the value of love and compassion towards my fellow beings and to appreciate the rewards of encouraging and understanding others.

My children have now flown the nest to live and work in different parts of the world. I am able to concentrate fully on my work at my clinic, to consolidate all my experiences and knowledge and to continue to learn and develop my work further. It is a very stimulating time in my life and I feel a real sense of 'wholesomeness' which in turn has promoted a lot of creative energy.

Interestingly, just recently while working at my clinic I was drawn to a painting by Paul Klee entitled 'Main Road and Side Roads'.

The painting was presented to me by a dear school friend to celebrate the opening of my natural health clinic. It hangs on the wall of my therapy room and, although I had always admired it, I had come to accept it as part of the furniture. Looking at it now, the penny dropped. The painting reflected my own life in which there have been many side roads before rejoining the main road towards fulfilling my destiny as a natural health practitioner.

With the blessings of the universe, I would like to continue teaching and inspiring people how to live their life's purpose as best as I can. My violin is also beckoning me again.

Then there is another favourite occupation – to carry on with my third flying lessons.

My new mantra is:

> As I walk this Earth,
> I learn with open heart and mind.
> I walk in the knowledge that this is NOT the end.

The Rule of Life: DESIDERATA

GO PLACIDLY AMID THE NOISE AND HASTE, AND REMEMBER WHAT PEACE THERE MAY BE IN SILENCE.

As far as possible, without surrender, be on good terms with all persons. Speak your truth quietly and clearly and listen to others, even the dull and ignorant; they too have their story.

-

Avoid loud and aggressive persons; they are vexations to the spirit. If you compare yourself with others, you may become vain and bitter; for always there will be greater and lesser persons than yourself.

-

Keep interested in your own career, however humble; it is a real possession in the changing fortunes of time. Exercise caution in your business affairs for the world is full of trickery. But let this not blind you to what virtue there is; many persons strive for high ideals; and everywhere life is full of heroism.

-

Be yourself. Especially, do not feign affection. Neither be cynical about love for in the face of all aridity and disenchantment it is perennial as the grass.

-

Take kindly the counsel of the years, gracefully surrendering the things of youth. Nurture strength of spirit to shield you in sudden misfortune. But do not distress yourself with imaginings. Many fears are born of fatigue and loneliness. Beyond a wholesome discipline, be gentle with yourself.

You are a child of the universe, no less than the trees and the stars; you have a right to be here. And whether or not it is clear to you, no doubt the universe is unfolding as it should.

Therefore be at peace with God, whatever you conceive Him to be, and whatever your labors and aspirations, in the noisy confusion of life keep peace with your soul.

With all its sham, drudgery and broken dreams, it is still a beautiful world. Be careful. Strive to be happy.

FOUND IN OLD SAINT PAUL'S CHURCH,
BALTIMORE, dated 1692

Whenever the 'going' is hard, may the wisdom of Desiderata help to give you stability and strength. It worked for me every time. I hope it does the same for you!

Acknowledgements

To my dear friend and mentor Ken, a teacher and poet. I asked him whether he would like to read through the draft of my new book, 'The Ten Qualities', to check my proficiency in English. Instead, he prompted me to look back at my childhood to help me understand how I arrived at where I am now.

Many months later, at the time of writing this and after we shared an emotional journey together, I find myself publishing 'The Ten Qualities' at the same time as this book. Thank you for your persistence, Ken and for encouraging me to think deeply about my childhood and to revive past memories.

This odyssey of my journey was no mean feat. I am most appreciative and thankful for your kindness, patience, encouragement, your wisdom and vision and sense of humour. Ken, be careful in future when you next get chatting to strange women after Pilates!

Thanks too go to Tom Evans, the wizard of words, and so many other things, who so skillfully takes the ethereal and grounds it onto the physical plane. Thank you for being a friend, neighbour and constant source of wisdom and encouragement.

About the Author

In this autobiography, Maya Kraus shares her life's endless travels on 'side roads' until finally reaching her potential – that of a well-sought-after therapist and healer.

She is an instructor for Touch for Health (kinesiology) which she has taught to many thousands of students. Her other qualifications are in reflexology, acupuncture, iridology, naturopathy, Chinese acupressure massage and bio-energy healing. She has appeared both on television abroad and on radio at home. She has a doctorate in complementary medicine and is a member of the Doctor/Healer Network.

On finally having reached her 'main road', she now runs the successful Castle Street Clinic in Guildford, Surrey, with her team of over twenty practitioners.

Her speciality is in dealing with anxieties, phobias and lack of self-esteem by removing old childhood patterning and achieving a positive attitude of self-empowerment. She is also experienced in working with allergies and detoxification of hidden viruses and toxins, for which she uses dowsing and kinesiology.

She also gained a performance diploma for violin from the London College of Music.

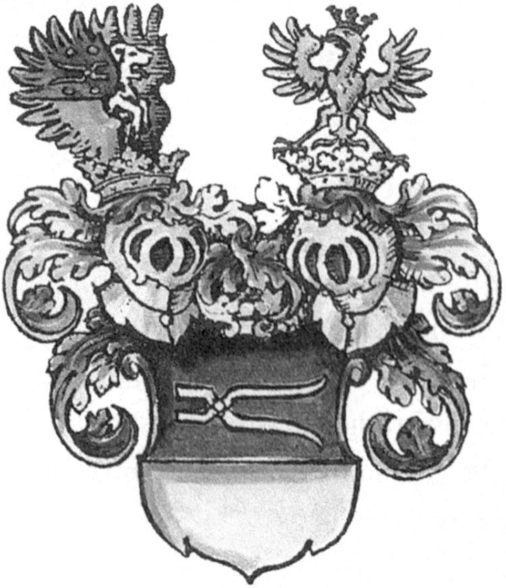

The Ten Qualities

The Ten Qualities is one of those books that comes along every now and then that makes you stop and really think. Our health and vitality is something we have an amazing degree of control over as many dis-eases are seeded in the mind.

By changing our attitude to life, we literally change our demeanour both internally and externally. Stress and childhood trauma play a big part too.

Maya Kraus has crafted a simple guidebook in two balanced parts. The first part describes the Ten Qualities themselves and how to use them. The second part of the book is brimming with simple ways we can improve our beingness and so achieve a freedom in our lives that often proves elusive.

This book will leave you with one lasting thought...

"I am free to be me!"

The Ten Qualities is available on Amazon:
ISBN 978-1-849-14277-9
You can also buy a personally signed copy from:
www.castlestreetclinic.co.uk

Ten Qualities

A Simple Guide to Well-Being
With 100 Inspiring Affirmations

Maya Kraus

Author of The Journey of a Healer

About Castle Street Clinic

The clinic was established in 1994 by director Maya Kraus. It quickly became a centre of excellence in natural health therapies, with over 30 different therapies on offer. It is pleasantly located near the town centre and the beautiful castle grounds.

It provides help and support for particular ailments and real treats if you just want to unwind and spoil yourself like aromatherapy or reflexology.

The body's own capacity to heal itself is often underestimated. Natural health therapies aim to encourage self-healing processes, thereby allowing the body to achieve optimum good health. To take your first step on the road to well-being, drop in or get in touch.

Visit: www.castlestreetclinic.com

or call 01483 300400

CASTLE STREET CLINIC
Guildford Natural Health Centre